WHERE DO
DEMONS LIVE?

About the Author

Born in Heliopolis, Egypt, Frater U∴D∴ has been working within the magical tradition for decades. He lived in Africa and Asia and trained with yoga and tantra masters, and studied languages and literature at the universities of Bonn and Lisbon. He is recognized as the founder of Pragmatic Magic and Ice Magic, and has written articles for many magazines, including *Unicorn*, *Thelema: Magazine for Magic and Tantra*, *Anubis*, *The Lamp of Thoth*, and *Chaos International*. His published works include *Practical Sigil Magic*, *High Magic*, and *High Magic II*. Among his translations are the books of Peter Carroll and Ramsey Dukes, and Aleister Crowley's *Book of Lies*. At present, he lives in Belgium, where he is the CEO of a software-development company.

WHERE DO DEMONS LIVE?

EVERYTHING YOU WANT TO KNOW ABOUT MAGIC

FRATER U∴ D∴

TRANSLATED BY MELINDA KUMBALEK

Llewellyn Publications
Woodbury, Minnesota

First Edition
First Printing, 2010

First published in German in 2005, as *Wo wohnen die Dämonen? Was Sie schon immer über Magie wissen wollten,* by the publishing house Wilhelm Heyne Verlag.
Cover art © Digital Stock
Cover design by Kevin R. Brown
Editing by Brett Fechheimer
Translated from German by Melinda Kumbalek

Llewellyn is a registered trademark of Llewellyn Worldwide, Ltd.

Library of Congress Cataloging-in-Publication Data
U. D., Frater, 1952–
 [Wo wohnen die Dämonen? English]
 Where do demons live? : everything you want to know about magic / Frater
U. D. ; translated by Melinda Kumbalek. — 1st ed.
  p. cm.
 ISBN 978-0-7387-1479-0
 1. Magic. I. Title.
 BF1613.U1413 2010
 133.4'3—dc22
                    2009039382

Llewellyn Publications
A Division of Llewellyn Worldwide, Ltd.
2143 Wooddale Drive, Dept. 978-0-7387-1479-0
Woodbury, Minnesota 55125-2989, U.S.A.
www.llewellyn.com

Printed in the United States of America

Other Books by Frater U∴D∴

High Magic

High Magic II

Practical Sigil Magic

Secrets of Western Sex Magic

Preliminary Note

At workshops and seminars, and in numerous conversations with fellow magicians, Frater U∴ D∴ is often asked some very interesting questions about magic and the occult. Since many of these questions can be answered with fairly short explanations, he decided that a magical question-and-answer format would be just the right method to respond to these queries.

And who would be more qualified at answering such questions than our chatty old sorceress Aunt Klara, Frater U∴ D∴'s humorously fierce alter ego? She has been sitting at her antique writing desk now for ages, just sipping away at her coffee and chain-smoking. The desk, with its jet-black, crocheted tablecloth, was part of the estate of an old archbishop who was guillotined during the French Revolution. Aunt Klara sits there, answering questions and giving advice on practical magic and much more, providing both historical and current information that cannot be found anywhere else.

No wonder, then, that readers of the German magic magazine *Anubis* kept Aunt Klara busy with their questions, and her responses in the column "Aunt Klara's Temple of Solace"—reprinted here in their entirety—were always a favorite feature of the magazine.

Contents

Do I need a master?

I am a 27-year-old man, and I've got a problem: Magic has fascinated me for years and I have already read lots of books on the subject, but I'm having trouble actually getting started without a teacher or master. How should I go about finding one? After all, I don't want to make any mistakes.

Thomas B. from F.

Dear Thomas,

You are certainly not alone. Plenty of others out there are fascinated by magic but do not have the opportunity to receive any kind of formal training. Just remember: most magicians are self-taught! Don't be afraid to try! In other words, to become skilled at magic, you will just have to get off your butt and practice, practice, practice. No master can relieve you of the basic practical work that you will have to do, and no teacher can protect you from having to just dive headfirst into the cold water so that you can learn through "trial and error."

It is not a master that you need. What you really need is the courage to finally tackle the situation yourself. Martin Luther once said, "A despairing arse will never produce a happy fart." So don't be afraid to take risks and just try. Go out into the woods and do a pentagram ritual, invoke the spirits of the earth, or charge a sigil for magical power. Soon enough you will begin to realize that magic is headed your way with wide-open arms. *But you will have to grasp the opportunity yourself!*

If you are unsure about certain technical details in your magical practice, seek out others who might have more experience or attend a few workshops and seminars. And there are two things you should always remember: (1) When the student is ready, a master will appear on his own. At least that is what masters of the Orient always say. (2) A "master" is never much more than a catalyst anyway, one that triggers processes with only one ultimate goal—namely, to lead you to your actual, true master. And if you would like to sneak a glimpse of this true master already, just go into the bathroom and look in the mirror.

I will be watching!
Your Aunt Klara

SHOULD I JOIN A MAGICAL ORDER?

WOULD IT BE A GOOD IDEA TO JOIN A MAGICAL ORDER TO GET PROPER MAGICAL TRAINING?

KARIN D. FROM K.

Dear Karin,

Yes and no. Let me start with the no: most magical orders consist of only a handful of members with highly diversified qualifications. Thus, there is little time for the actual training of novices. After all, good teachers are scarce everywhere. The documents and secret archives of such orders are frequently nothing more than what you can find in any good book on magic (which are quite rare, too, by the way), and sometimes the authors of such books are members of these orders, too. All too often, a magical order is merely a group of drinking buddies with esoteric interests. So the disappointment can be great once a beginner starts to see beyond all that secretive fuss, and the true rabbit-breeder mentality starts to shine through that silken robe.

But there is another side to the coin that certainly speaks in favor of membership in a magical order— namely, its force field. Most beginners have trouble comprehending that the true task of an order is not to convey information, but rather to gradually bring its members into contact with a specific force field. (In this sense, grades and degrees are not really meant to be viewed as rewards for the successful completion of a certain course of study, but rather as milestones to define the tasks and goals that are yet to be completed or reached. Therefore one often refers to "fulfilling" a grade.) There is little to say about the force field of an order. You can only trust your instincts and intuition. As a rule of thumb: if you do not feel comfortable with its force field right from the start, then you should by all means consciously avoid all contact with that order. Maybe its energy is generally not compatible with yours, or maybe it is just not the right time to make contact.

All the best,
Aunt Klara

DOES MAGIC ALWAYS HAVE TO BE RITUALISTIC?

DOES MAGIC ALWAYS HAVE TO BE SO RITUALISTIC? I SIMPLY CANNOT STAND ALL THE DRAMATIC FUSS; I FIND IT QUITE RIDICULOUS AND IT REALLY GETS ON MY NERVES. IT IS ACTUALLY QUITE REVOLTING.

PETER Z. FROM W.

Dear Peter,

Ritual magic is just one of the many branches of the magical arts. For example, when a magician charges a sigil or travels into a tattwa realm, it really does not have much to do with ritual in the technical sense of the word. The same applies to other magical workings, such as astral travel or healing with a magic mirror. However, with your expression *dramatic fuss*, I feel inclined to raise a finger here in warning.

Just what is a ritual anyway? It is the dramaturgical interpretation of a magical act of will and the choreography of magical energy movements, as Frater U∴ D∴ always preaches. We should remember that the subconscious mind is considered to be the main source of magical power (*magis*), and that it likes to think in imagery and sensory stimuli and does not care one bit about a cultivated sense of aesthetic appeal. It is like a small child demanding clear, bold colors, pompous sentimentality, emotionalism, and eye-rolling exaggeration. The good ole ritual magician is aware of this and will play the role of Caesar when Caesar is called for— clear, bold colors, sappy sentimentality, and so on and so forth. Then the subconscious mind will promptly join in the fun and do everything in its power to bring about the object of desire. (By the way, this is exactly the reason why rituals of thanks are important. They act as a reward for the subconscious—like psychological PR work, in a sense.)

One cynic once said that no one has ever lost any money by underestimating the taste of American audiences. And that does not just apply to American audiences, but also and especially to the subconscious mind. So be careful with such judgments and have a little more respect for the child inside of you. After all, it showers you with an abundance of gifts day after day. No one will ever force you to perform rituals, but please take a minute to think about the principles that they incorporate. Also keep in mind that rituals fulfill the need of *religio* that many people have, as well as the need to perform holy acts—and both of these needs are rooted very deeply. As far as the rest goes, remember that not all rituals are the same; you can certainly write more "aesthetic" scripts if that is what you prefer. As long as these are not over-intellectualized, the universe that we call the subconscious mind will like just about anything.

That is all the preaching for now.
Aunt Klara

IS THE MAGICAL PATH COMPATIBLE WITH EASTERN PHILOSOPHIES?

WHERE CAN I READ UP ON THE DIFFERENCES BETWEEN EASTERN WAYS, SUCH AS THOSE FOLLOWED IN INDIA, AND THE VARIOUS MAGICAL PATHS? WHAT IS THE GENERAL DIFFERENCE BETWEEN EASTERN AND WESTERN TECHNIQUES? I AM A BIT WORRIED ABOUT "MISIDENTIFICATION" HERE. HOW CAN I GAIN SOME FAST AND EFFECTIVE INSIGHT INTO THE SUBJECT? CAN THE MAGICAL PATH EVER BE THE WRONG ONE? MAYBE IT IS EVEN BETTER THAN THE WAY OF ZEN?

MANFRED K. FROM F.

Dear Manfred,

Boy oh boy, that is quite an avalanche of questions. Well, then, here we go! On to your first question: I have no idea where you came up with the notion that *Eastern* and *magical* are so different, and I can assure you that there is not a whole lot of literature out there that would discuss something like that. Maybe you have been fooled by the common misconception that only Eastern paths can be mystical, while Western ones are "magical." Now that is certainly not true, as can clearly be seen in the numerous magical systems within Taoism, such as the ancient Tibetan religion Bon and Hindu Tantrism, just to name a few. All of these are strongly influenced by shamanic elements and therefore can quite accurately be described as "magical."

The common misconception that I mentioned above is based on something quite ordinary—namely, on the way these Eastern mystical systems are presented to us: after all, their language, customs, and culture are very foreign to us Westerners. Thus, we have to rely on others to convey these foreign concepts to us, and as far as that is concerned, the old rule of thumb applies: "First come, first served." For example, some people are utterly flustered when they encounter magicians who only work with five chakras instead of seven. The only reason for this is the mere fact that much more literature about the seven-chakra system has been translated into Western languages than about the numerous other Eastern chakra systems. (There are even systems that work with 64 or 144 chakras, for example.)

Due to the lack of information, people often mistakenly believe that there can only be one "true" system. And due to such a lack of information, a person of Western society automatically thinks that such Eastern ways are always mystical. But we should keep in mind that there is no such thing as the one and only Eastern path, just as no single Western path exists either.

The techniques of both systems are principally the same, with only a few major differences once you look past all the culturally specific frills. The names of the deities (or demons) invoked or evoked are different, as are the basic ritual structures and secondary disciplines at times. Chinese magicians, for example, do not use much astrology in their work (if Chinese astrology can be compared at all to our Western concept of the term; instead, it is more like a type of daily and yearly divination similar to that of the ancient Egyptians), and they also do not use any symbols from the Hebrew Kabbalah. Instead, the symbolism of the I Ching plays a large role.

But despite all of the superficial differences, the fundamental principles of magic are almost always the same. Formulas such as "will + imagination + trance = magic" are valid worldwide—from the illiterate shamans of Siberia or the Upper Amazon basin to the literary magic of the European Faust books or the Muslim magic of the Koran.

It is interesting that you mention the word *misidentification*, though. You are probably referring to the fundamental statement that many Eastern systems make: namely, that our world is *Maya*, which is often incorrectly translated as "illusion." Incorrect in the sense that this so-called "illusion" is very real and therefore significant. The old master Aleister Crowley put this quite nicely once: "The whole universe is an illusion, but it is an illusion difficult to get rid of."

"Misidentification" could therefore occur by denying the illusionary nature of creation and convincing oneself of being something that is steady and constant, or non-illusionary. (A Taoist would say—convincing oneself that anything stable at all can exist apart from change.)

But sometimes magic is also called the "art of illusion." Just take a look at the tarot card The Magician, which was commonly called "The Juggler" in earlier times. The magician is considered to be a master of illusion who plays with these illusions like a juggler at a fair; this, however, does not imply that the results of magic are nothing but lies and deception (although skeptics might hope that were true!). The results are only *relative*, just like everything else. "Fast and effective" insight can be gained primarily through everyday practical magic. After all, its sole objective is to achieve results. Either you are able to perform magic, or you are not. If you approach it empirically like this, then you will not be able to fool yourself.

On the other hand, dear Manfred K., I have the impression that you are more concerned about receiving a so-called "absolute" answer. You are probably a mystically oriented person—otherwise you would not have asked that last question at all. So I will certainly answer that question for you. Yes, of course, the magical path may indeed be unsuitable for some people. That is actually more often the rule than the exception. Without praising ourselves too much here, we can safely say that magicians have always been part of a tiny, elite circle—despite the fact that many clergy members like to claim that the opposite is true. If you ever point out to a Catholic priest the demonstrably shamanic elements of the Holy Communion, the sacraments, or other holy acts (necromancy, the spirits in "fetishes," and even a sort of god-cannibalism, or theophagy), he will certainly be quite annoyed. In fact, he would probably be thoroughly appalled if you would go so far as to describe magic as the "mother" instead of the "problem child" of (his!) religion.

Magic is all about "doing," about taking action and being active. The magician takes control of his or her own destiny. Which is why a magician can even be an atheist, although this is usually the exception. The magician strives to conquer the Kingdom of Heaven with his or her own two hands. The mystic, on the contrary, is of a more contemplative nature and puts his or her faith in the grace of God. (One could also say that the mystic is less of a rebel than the magician, and prefers obedience. After all, there is a good reason why the "patron saint" of Western magic is Lucifer, the bringer of light, who defiantly shouts his *"non serviam!"* at his Demiurge—mystics would view this as an unheard-of act of insubordination.)

To wrap things up, just keep this in mind: Zen and magic do not exclude one another at all—on the contrary. For example, if you work with the "active Way of Zen" as practiced in Asian martial arts, then your head will be full of stories about the magical skills of martial-arts masters. It is pretty much the same with zazen. Basically, there is just one single maxim: "Do what thou wilt—but do it right!" And every magician should be able to agree with that, don't you think?

Of course, if you would rather meditate than perform magic, then by all means do so. As I already said, not everyone is born to be a magician, and it would be silly to attempt to judge people's dispositions. No single path is better than another (or more "holy" or more "true" or any other silly adjective that those theologians—esoteric ones, too!—can come up with).

Now, please do not ask me which path you should take. That is really entirely up to you. And anyway, I am late for my coffee with the ladies . . .

Aunt Klara

Are some orders really as old as they claim?

Many books on magic talk about a magical tradition of ancient alliances and brotherhoods that have supposedly existed in secret since the days of Atlantis. Is there any truth to this?

Sigrid T. from A.

Dear Sigrid,

There may be a little or a lot of truth to this, depending on how you look at it.

Let us be honest. From an ordinary historical point of view, most of these claims are complete rubbish! It is difficult for many orders to resist the temptation of decorating themselves with ancient foreign feathers according to the belief that "old equals good." For example, there is a certain Rosicrucian organization that boldly claims that Socrates and Echnaton were once members. Theodor Reuss, who was—among so many other things—a notorious dealer of fake credentials, once convinced Rudolf Steiner to purchase a certain order's charter for 1,500 reichsmarks (which was a lot of money back then!). That purchase helped Steiner become Rex Summus X° of the O.T.O. long before "Good Ole 666" Aleister Crowley ever even joined the order!

And even the Golden Dawn had the audacity to falsify documents (and quite clumsily at that) in order to supposedly "prove" its legitimacy. This obsession with legitimacy, however, seems quite silly to members of the younger generation, who are often quite critical of their own backgrounds and family dogmas and no longer hold the opinion that everything that is old and passed down must automatically be good. Moreover, to use the example of the Golden Dawn again, an order with an otherwise excellent concept may crumble to pieces because of unnecessary stumbling blocks—like the exposure of such a swindle.

In places where there are gaps in an order's history, crazy stories of a "spiritual affinity" or even "reincarnation" are sometimes concocted to give the whole thing more authority. Along the way, dubious sources are often cited to support these stories, such as the "secret archives of the Vatican." Since the papal state never really denies anything as a rule, this is a surefire method, especially considering the fact that there always have been and always will be people who will fall for something like this. (So much for the negative side of the coin . . .)

As with everything else in life, there is also a bright side. And in order to comprehend it, we need to understand that truthfulness in the everyday sense of the word is not always a virtue in magic. After all, magic is also the application of mythology and symbolism, and mythological or symbolical truths cannot always be equaled with the objective facts of science. But that does not necessarily make them untrue! (An anecdote functions in a similar manner. It, too, does not necessarily have to describe a "true event." It is sufficient enough if it could be true or plausible, and if it accurately describes the person's character according to the common consensus.) And why should we as magicians, with an interest in transcending time and space, hesitate to tell stories? Especially considering the fact that since such stories are always subjective, they are told and listened to in a highly critical way, and consequently reinvented and adapted from generation to generation.

Just remember two things: (a) do not confuse the various levels with one another, and (b) do not lose sight of the practical value. Not confusing the levels means: do not consciously use deception or trickery and do not turn myths into objective facts, since this would automatically depreciate their practical value. This, in turn, would fulfill the expectations that such a world view has to offer.

It is a well-known fact that many shamans rave about the "good ole days" when magicians were much more powerful than they are today. This is a typically human way of explaining away the past, and also a means of blocking the censor. By firmly believing that people could levitate in the past, it makes being able to levitate now much easier, since we principally believe that it can be done. Indeed, some people tend to avoid the strenuous task of even thinking at all, by holding beliefs such as "I stand in the true current of wisdom," or simpler yet, "It has always been like that." But of course this can work like a double-edged knife. On the other hand, the time-related distance that this creates with the present in connection with a projection onto other entities ("masters," the "high" or "initiated," "mahatmas," and so forth) and the related subordination or surrendering of the ego all combine to release magical abilities that would otherwise remain untapped.

Of course, my simple little column here might cause all followers of the true, pure, and ancient traditional teachings to go mad, assuming they would get the foolish little notion to read it at all. And in no way do I mean any of the above in a derogatory sense. Karl Marx is claimed to have once said that truth is whatever is useful to a person. And that applies in particular to magic. So whoever needs a glorious past in order to work better magically should feel free to create one. Experience shows, however, that placing such importance on history is more of a pitfall than an asset, since it causes a tendency to appreciate the outer form more than the inner essence.

To wrap things up, let me summarize as follows: if time is an illusion, then we should also use it as raw material for our telesmatic actions, such as our outlook on life, beliefs, matter, spirit, magical power, and so on. But we should only do it out of a sense of inner freedom and with the awareness that we as magicians are capable of doing absolutely anything that we really want to—and that includes the invention of biological or spiritual ancestors.

And now, my practical advice: If you come across an order whose rituals and knowledge supposedly stem back to the days of Osiris without any gaps, then please take a very close look and see how serious that claim is. And if an order tries to make your mouth water with the claim to have evidence in the form of "secret documents" that are, unfortunately, only available to the higher grades and degrees, then you can safely make a black mark next to this organization's name in the honesty category—although that does not automatically mean you might not be able to learn something there. Just don't expect to be welcomed with open arms if you let them know that you've caught on to their little game.

And now I have an appointment with my old Incan aunt from back in the days of Atlantis to plot the future fate of the world . . .

All the best from your dreadfully knowledgeable
Aunt Klara

WHAT DO YOU THINK OF FRANZ BARDON?

DEAR AUNT KLARA! TELL ME, WHAT DO YOU THINK ABOUT FRANZ BARDON'S SYSTEM (KABBALAH, ETC.)? I HOPE MY QUESTION WILL NOT CAUSE YOU ANY SLEEPLESS NIGHTS WHILE CHEWING ON YOUR FINGERNAILS.

GÜNTHER F. FROM W.

Dear Günther,

Thank you very much for being so concerned about my manicure. (Why didn't you ask if my toenails might curl at your question?) But don't worry, I have experienced worse than that in my fifty-plus magical years. Seriously now: of course there is no objective way of saying what I think about Franz Bardon and his magic, so what you are probably looking for is my personal opinion. Well, that opinion would be quite mixed. Frater U∴ D∴ liked to criticize Bardon for his dogmatic approach, and as a result angry Bardonians retorted by calling him a "naïve scribbler" and a "charlatan," but that is the fate of all those who have ever dared to trample on someone else's honor. It also shows how important Bardon still is today, which certainly cannot be the result of a mere misunderstanding.

But what makes Bardon so great and so controversial at the same time? In order to understand this, we have to dig way back into the past and try to view this magician within the context of his era. Without a doubt he has given us a magical system that is both comprehensive and cohesive. In addition, he has taken great pains to write in a style that is clearly understandable—a fact that is greatly appreciated by many.

Back when Bardon's books were first published (I can still remember . . . it was in the early 1950s, and we were simply starving for good literature on magic), they presented a true bright light on the horizon. They saved us the trouble of having to gather everything from various obscure sources, and Bardon presented us with the legend of a "high initiate" who is finally able to explain everything. The fact that this "everything" did not go all that deep was easily overlooked in the vast quantity of material that he presented, and hardly anyone noticed that many "explanations" were actually more like "transfigurations." After all, you always knew what to expect with Bardon: like no other serious author of books about magic (and he can still be considered that today), he made a clear distinction between good and evil, right and wrong.

However, we tend to get smarter with time, so when bold questions are asked and we get nothing but smart answers in return, or the questions are avoided altogether, we also tend to get more skeptical and critical. Not that his system would not work—it does indeed for many people, and often too well, at that! But in the end, that is true of all magical systems that are self-contained and cohesive. To make a long story short: Bardon is especially well suited for beginners wanting an excellent introduction to magic. Unfortunately, though, he also makes sure that the beginner remains a beginner for a very long time (if not forever) as a result of fanatical thoroughness. He does this by means of constant warnings and admonitions, and by providing exercise guidelines that are in principle correct, but on the whole entirely unrealistic and unnecessary. His first step alone can easily take ten to thirty years, and that is still a far cry from actual magic. Some of his exercises are excellent, as long as you ignore his instructions about practice time.

But personally, I do not like Bardon's silly, patriarchal manner. There is no doubt that he accomplished great things in his time, but considering the vibrant intelligence of a certain Aleister Crowley or the grim intensity and uncompromising originality of a certain Austin Osman Spare, Bardon is merely a small light in comparison. He never made any "spiritual quantum leaps," and could never hold a light even to his teacher Rah Omir Quintscher. He was an archivist and a compiler, a bookworm by nature who wanted to make his own visions binding for others—which he succeeded in doing for a fairly long time, at least in German-speaking areas.

To contemporary novice magicians, however, Bardon's dogmatism often proves to be disastrous. One could even say that his books (in contrast to those of the other magicians previously mentioned) already seem to be quite outdated. He sets rules where none are necessary, points out restrictions where none actually exist, and intimidates where words of encouragement and consolation would be much more effective. When reading his words, one has the impression that he is really not interested in having his students make any progress. Instead, he seems more concerned with basking in his own glory, which of course seems quite fake and conveys a false impression. Surely every good magician has a tendency toward self-adulation; after all, this is a natural characteristic of a strong (but not necessarily "mature") personality. But Bardon as a person remains inaccessible to the reader. Instead, any personalized aspect is stifled by moral preaching and bigotry, and Bardon never mentions a word about his own practice apart from vague insinuations.

I could go on forever in this manner, but let us forget about all of that and just say that Bardon is a well-known brother-in-kind whom we should finally see off into a well-deserved retirement. After all, if you scratch on the surface too much, don't be surprised if the whole wall comes crumbling down upon you . . .

A bumped and bruised
Aunt Klara

WHAT ABOUT KARMIC REPERCUSSIONS AND TAPPING SPIRITS?

DEAR AUNT KLARA, HOW HAVE YOU BEEN DOING LATELY? I HAVE A FEW MORE QUESTIONS FOR YOU TODAY THAT I HOPE YOU CAN ANSWER FOR ME:

1. WHAT ABOUT THE KARMIC REPERCUSSIONS THAT CAN SUPPOSEDLY OCCUR WHEN MAGIC IS USED TO HARM OTHERS?

2. IT HAS BEEN REPORTED THAT MADAME BLAVATSKY COULD CAUSE TAPPING NOISES TO OCCUR AND THAT WAS CONSIDERED PROOF OF HER OCCULT SKILLS (COLIN WILSON). BUT WHAT ABOUT A "RATTLING" NOISE

IN THE WALL THAT OCCURS RHYTHMICALLY THREE TIMES IN A ROW ON VARIOUS OCCASIONS? COULD IT BE AN ASTRAL BEING (IF SO, WHAT KIND?), AN EXTERNAL PRODUCT OF MAGIC OR THE REFLECTION OF A CERTAIN COMPLEX THAT AUTONOMOUSLY SPLINTERED OFF (SPLIT PERSONALITY, SO-CALLED "SEMIS")? OF WHAT NATURE ARE THESE NOISES AND HOW SHOULD A PERSON DEAL WITH THEM? (OR SHOULD AN EXORCIST BE CALLED IN, OR MAYBE A POPE?)

MANFRED K. FROM F.

Dear Manfred,

Thank you, my dear, I am doing as well as can be expected—as the lie goes. (What other options are there, really?) Since you are already an old acquaintance, so to speak, I have grown used to having to reword your questions a bit more clearly on my own. How else could I understand what you mean when you vaguely ask, "What about the karmic repercussions"?

It is quite simple: karma is the law of cause and effect. Do you agree? When I attack someone with my magic and give it my all, then I have created the cause and will therefore reap the effect. So, what form does this effect take? Ha ha ha, well, that is exactly where the problem begins! In nearly all metaphysical considerations, one very simple fact is overlooked: the effect that I reap (the "karma") is nothing but the fact that someone else gets everything that I have dished out, provided that my work was successful. And that is that. End of the definition.

Just as Frater U.·. D.·. says in his studies on combat magic, I also feel that it is a disastrous mistake to believe that there is some kind of cosmic authority that will slap us on the hand in punishment. It might be nice if it really did work like that, but apart from the visions of those "afterlife New Agers" there is no evidence of anything like this whatsoever. In other words, although the law of cause and effect certainly does exist (at least in the pre-Heisenbergian universe), there is no such thing as moral categorization, as any Buddhist teacher will confirm.

In any case, this belief can be disastrous for the main reason that it distracts us from the fact that we are responsible for protecting ourselves when we are attacked. Although working with a higher authority (guardian angel, clan totem, and so on) can indeed make a person invulnerable to a certain extent, this requires a great deal of preliminary practical groundwork. Mere wishful thinking is simply not enough! During a magical attack, there is nothing worse than having a false sense of security. After all, magical energies are often very subtle and like to "sneak in through the back door," so it is absolutely necessary to deal with them technically and without bias. The so-called "karma" that so-called "black magic" causes is actually an entirely different story.

On the one hand, it could be caused by the bad conscience that often accompanies such an operation. This can become a bad spearhead that may turn against the attacking magician. The results (often subconscious in nature) can take the form of self-punishment mechanisms that can bring about a sort of Pyrrhic victory in which both parties, the perpetrator *and* the victim, end up grumpily moping about.

But there are also magical protection tools that can cause the invasive energy to bounce back to the perpetrator like a good deflection shield. If the assailant does not expect something like this to happen, a magical backfire can occur, meaning that one's own magic can boomerang right back. But of course that is merely a technical problem that can certainly be avoided by taking appropriate precautionary measures. After all, magical combat can escalate quickly, resulting at least temporarily in extreme paranoia for both parties. For this reason, all experienced combat magicians will agree that magical warfare should always be the very last option (just like in the military). This is all the more true when you realize that a magical war waged by individuals demands the accomplishment of tasks that not even an entire army could fulfill. Not until you have considered all of these aspects should you be worried about karma as a "bank account in the afterlife" and about the consequences for a possible later incarnation (if you believe in such a thing)—and really not until then! Help yourself, then God will help you.

Now, on to your second question: honestly, I do not care one bit about whether a poltergeist knocks five times or rattles three times. What I notice in the wording of your question, though, is something entirely different, namely the misconception that being able to cause paranormal phenomena is supposedly proof of occult skills. You have obviously gotten that from Colin Wilson. But there is also evidence that good ole HPB (Helena P. Blavatsky) sometimes applied a few tricks of her own when things did not go as planned. And when her tricks were exposed, it caused her to lose the head position in the Theosophical Society, which she had founded.

Plus, never confuse magic with psi. Although psi phenomena are a part of everyday magical life, the magician should give them as little attention as a yogi gives to his siddhis. What use is it if you can bend a spoon with the power of your mind, but you can never get a parking space with magic during rush hour? Or if you can never see beyond the tip of your nose and are not able to grow and develop?

But I am not trying to avoid your question here, so I would like to say a few words about the rattling noises. Are we dealing with astral beings, or complexes that have autonomously splintered off? Well, how should I know that? But seriously: both cases are nothing but labels that do not really provide any explanations. What on earth actually is a "complex that has autonomously splintered off"? Who splinters off what, how, and why? Even Thomas Mann let himself be satisfied with such lame pseudo-explanations as "magically objectivized wishful thinking on the part of the medium," although he personally attended Schrenck-Notzing's séances! Let's just accept the fact that we simply do not know exactly what magic we are dealing with here. The hypothesis about astral spirits is no better or worse than those pseudo-scientific monster words used by Jung. In any case, none of the theories can be proved.

That leads us to the question of how to deal with such phenomena. Here it can once again be considered a blessing that the occult doctrines in dealing with the "unexplained" have brought about new technology that is meanwhile millennia old. The possibilities are numerous, and although I cannot go into detail about everything here, your reference to exorcism is certainly appropriate. Although I dare to doubt whether a pope is the right man to do the job, unless a very Christian household is involved. Pete Carroll once wrote that usually only the residents themselves have to be exorcized and not their homes, and that is quite true. Often poltergeists occur around teenagers in puberty, and also where mentally disabled or mentally retarded people live. My own observations have shown that people with strong sexual frustrations often trigger such phenomena as well.

A skilled magician, a shaman, or a trained witch can all eliminate such occurrences with ease by harmonizing or treating the person who is triggering the occurrences. In very rare cases, a spirit trap must be constructed and set off, but this should really be left to highly experienced magicians who ideally should be skilled in psychology and human relations as well.

Haunted greetings,
Your Aunt Klara

Can a magical operation be considered a success if the result has already occurred?

Dear Aunt Klara, what do you think about a magical operation that was a success, but then later information revealed that the desired result had already occurred long before the magical act was performed?

Diego S. from H.

Dear Diego,

Your question touches right on a sore spot that, on the other hand, is also a truly fascinating aspect of magic. A sore spot insofar as that the "true reasons" for such phenomena are beyond our comprehension. Since you unfortunately failed to mention a practical example, I will do it for you. Aleister Crowley once wanted to receive a letter from a friend who I believe lived in Australia. It was a very important letter. When Crowley was tired of waiting, he performed an appropriate ritual. A few days later, he received the desired letter. Curiously, though, the letter had been written and sent a few days *before* the ritual was performed (intercontinental mail service was quite slow at the time).

There are several possible models of explanation for such occurrences. The simplest and therefore probably the most appealing explanation would be that it was principally a divination: the magician intuitively senses that a certain event is imminent and acts instinctively in order to "bring it about." The question is, however, whether or not the desired result would have occurred without prior triggering by the ritual. (For example, the letter could have been lost.) Of course, there is no way to ever be sure, but in any case there are some magicians who will advise you to always perform the ritual anyway, even if the desired result has already occurred *before the ritual actually takes place*. That at least has the advantage that the matter can be ultimately concluded by using the symbolic language of the subconscious mind. A religious person would possibly perform a ritual of thanks.

Modern magic is increasingly interested in getting to the bottom of this phenomenon of "retroactive magic," as it is technically called. After all, we modern magicians live in a world that is filled with science fiction and stories about travels through time in which even physicists calculate time "backwards." If magic really is only the *directing of information* (and many things support this), and if information exists beyond the boundaries of space *and* time and can be transferred (after all, it does not contain matter and possibly not even energy), then we can see various models of explanation flashing on the horizon that could knock an old aunt like me, permanent wave and all, right off her feet.

Then the question is: Can we change the past with magic? Can we (afterwards, mind you!) shift the switches of time? Honestly, I am quite hesitant to propose such a profound, reality-shattering claim. But if, and I repeat *if*, this were actually true, then retroactive magic would actually be "memories of the future"—a concept that would make the space gods and UFOs of Charroux and Däniken seem like harmless garden gnomes in comparison.

If the magician—as often claimed and repeatedly confirmed by magic's practitioners—actually can change reality, if this reality exists beyond time and space, and if we can succeed in giving this claim a theoretical and practical, applicable, examinable foundation, then it probably would not be exaggerating to say that we are currently about to make the largest spiritual quantum leap in the entire history of humanity in the field of magic (and not only there).

My dear Diego, I am very sorry that I was only able to answer your question with numerous other questions. But don't take it too hard. Our time is certainly not up yet, and if the current development within the magic scene lives up to just half of what it promises, soon the kind of magic we call our own will surely be magic as humanity has never before known it.

Here's to the pioneering spirit!

Hurrah!

Aunt Klara

WHERE DO DEMONS LIVE?

DEAR AUNT KLARA, ONE QUESTION HAS BEEN BOTHERING ME FOR YEARS—TO BE MORE SPECIFIC, EVER SINCE I BEGAN EXPERIMENTING WITH EVOCATIONS. WHERE DO DEMONS LIVE?

PETRA H. FROM Z.

Dear Petra,

Oh boy, did you catch me off guard with that one! Hmm, where *do* they live? After several sleepless nights, I finally realized that this question is not as strange, trite, or even funny as it first seems. You are probably hinting at the endless debate between animists and spiritists that still gets people (e.g., parapsychologists) quite worked up. The animists believe that demons (and all other "seemingly transcendental beings") are actually psychological projections, meaning that they originate within the magician himself or herself.

On the other hand, the spiritists claim that demons are real, self-sufficient entities that would exist even without our help. According to the animists, then, these flaky lads reside in your own soul, whereas the spiritists insist that they live in the astral world (or in a similar place; the different levels of the various systems are so numerous that it's hard to keep track of them all). Neither group can scientifically prove its position, nor can either group disprove the position of the other. So, again, it is merely a question of how one views his or her own universe from an objective standpoint. Since a true modern magician is continually training his or her ability to smoothly shift from one paradigm to another, it doesn't matter much how things "really" are, especially considering the fact that the word *real* does not hold much value. If you would like a pragmatic approach, however, I can recommend the following:

Only view demons as real, existing beings when you are performing evocations (for example, when summoning demons to appear in a triangle you have created); at all other times, consider them to be merely an aspect of yourself. This method has three advantages: (a) when not performing ritual work, you are not susceptible to the pranks that these little devils like to play; (b) it ensures that demons will manifest more easily during your ritual work with the circle and triangle; (c) you will be training yourself to think flexibly, thus enabling a fast shift from one paradigm to another.

However, if you feel that you can ignore my advice, then I can only say the following: if you really do conjure a demon and it manifests, it always feels like a real, autonomous being, regardless of what your common sense might have to say about it. Admittedly, an experience like that will probably make you tremble in your robe, and the energy produced by fear is exactly what makes such manifestation possible in the first place. But if a demon appears and you think, "Ha! You are nothing but a projection of the dark side of my soul" and you feel incredibly clever in doing so, just like C. G. Jung himself, then that is nothing but foolishness—and you are obviously much

more interested in supporting your intellectual concept than having a true demonic experience. Maybe
you are just scared? After all, demons are not the kind
of guys that a sensible aunt would want to have at
her tea party. Explaining your way out of things may
work to banish them, but it will not eliminate their
existence entirely.

With a demonic grin,
Aunt Klara

Is it a good idea to attend magic workshops?

I have noticed that there are a great number of workshops being offered on the subject of magic. Are such events beneficial or is it better to practice on one's own, for example with the help of books? Of course it is also a question of money. Such workshops are certainly not cheap.

Karl-Heinz R. from H.

Dear Karl-Heinz,

Well, it all depends on how disciplined and creative you are. Of course, it is always a good idea to make your own experiences. On the other hand, there is no point in wanting to reinvent the wheel time and again. Apart from all that, many books on magic are of doubtful quality at best and often only convey bits and pieces of information instead of coming right out with the whole truth. Although that can happen in a workshop as well. But a good teacher can save you years of meandering about on your own and wasting your money on expensive but useless books. A bad teacher, on the other hand, may either discourage or disappoint you, or literally send you running into the arms of booksellers and librarians. The stupid thing, though, is that you usually will not be able to tell which kind of teacher you are dealing with until after you have already spent a good deal of money to take part in the workshop.

So let me give you a few tips here that might help you to distinguish, ahead of time, a good workshop from a bad one:

1. The price is not the issue! A high fee is no guarantee of satisfactory performance. On the other

hand, unusually cheap seminars are often sales events in disguise, intended to market expensive products (e.g., special tools that the workshop organizers sell on commission), and there is also no guarantee that the lecturer will not be a fraud.

2. Always find out in advance the maximum number of people who will be allowed to participate in the workshop. Do not attend seminars with more than thirty participants if there is only one teacher. In situations like these, the participants usually do not get their fair share due to a lack of individual attention. Mass events of over fifty or even a hundred participants are only appropriate for lectures, but not for practical workshops that depend on the monitoring of one's progress and guidance by a teacher.

3. Carefully read all information available about the workshop. This should be obvious, but it is an aspect that is sometimes overlooked. Ask yourself if you really understand what the workshop is all about. Is the available information full of incomprehensible foreign words? Is the information too vague? Language can reveal lots of things! When in doubt, follow your

intuition. Or consult your pendulum or tarot cards to find the answer as to whether or not you should attend the workshop.

4. Pay close attention to the terms of cancellation; this is often the snag to such seminars. Although it is understandable that the event organizers should want to ensure a certain degree of commitment from the participants, it is nonetheless possible that a person might become sick or have another valid reason for cancellation. Only pay the full amount in advance as an exception and not as the rule; generally, no more than half in advance is appropriate.

Workshops present a number of advantages that should not be underestimated. You will meet like-minded people with various levels of knowledge. If you are open to the experience, you can get a number of ideas and suggestions from the various fields of esotericism, and about magic in particular. The continual exchange of ideas with other workshop participants makes even the dullest material enjoyable and lively. If you just happen to get an open-minded teacher who not only masters the trade but also enjoys what he or she is doing and has a certain degree of intuitive understanding, you might just be able to save many frustrating years of dabbling about on your own. And it never hurts to meet more like-minded practitioners.

However, do not attend too many workshops and seminars. Notorious "workshop hoppers" often have trouble internalizing the material, and the knowledge has no chance to really sink in. Such workshops—especially the good ones—need to be digested thoroughly. And eventually you should reach the point when you "outgrow" most workshops anyway and only attend certain events designed for specialists, where you can truly get some new input.

But there is one thing that even the absolute best teacher and most wonderful workshop will never be able to replace: your own practice and self-development. Never forget the fact that no encounter is coincidental, and that everyone gets the teacher that he or she deserves—meaning one whom the person can relate to, even if that merely takes the form of resistance against this teacher.

Greetings free of charge—but just this once!
Aunt Klara

How does one write magical music?

Hello Aunt Klara! The fact that music can trigger certain processes is self-evident. Music can influence the metabolism's regulatory system by means of rhythm and frequencies. The drums and rattles of the shamans are examples of tools used to induce states of trance (endorphins). How and according to what rules (if there are any out there based on practical experience) can "musick" be composed/structured in order to make it magically useful? Dilige et quod vis fac.

FRANK S. FROM I.

Dear Frank,

You certainly cannot expect me to present you with thorough, step-by-step instructions on how to write music. Even if I were able to (actually, I have no such knowledge whatsoever—at most I can play the radio), there would not be enough room here to allow for that. Nonetheless, I'd like to try to point out a few basic elements that might at least shed some light upon the subject of the magical use of music.

According to studies of pop music, the type of compositions that are most successful are those with rhythms that are closest to that of the human heartbeat. So that would at least be a good way to start. Ritual drum music (at least during the first few minutes) also works closely with the rhythm of the heart. The reason why this is so important, especially at the start of a magical operation, is explained by a simple psychological (sympathetic-magical) trick: namely, the fact that the involuntary bodily functions tend to react to external stimuli and to adapt to them if these external stimuli imitate the bodily functions first. In other words: if you begin by drumming to the rhythm of the heart and then slowly speed up the rhythm, the heartbeats of the listeners will automatically go faster, trying to catch up. (You can also influence a person by adapting your breathing rhythm to theirs, in a barely audible way, and then changing your own rhythm step by step. In nine out of ten cases, the victim will automatically adapt to your rhythm.) In this way, you can gradually bring the ritual participants into a trance, thus triggering the release of the body's own endorphins (also known as "brain opium"), as you correctly noted.

A monotonous rhythm is important here. Shamanic ritual music is namely quite monotone and repetitious. In addition, the sequence of sounds and rhythms should be kept relatively simple, and should reflect a certain tonal, rhythmic harmony; complicated jumps are difficult for both the organism and the mind to follow.

Now, there are still the factors of melody and volume. In magical music, melodies should also be kept simple—they should neither stir you up nor put you to sleep, although of course certain critical passages can be used to achieve certain effects. The melodies should correspond to the typical listening preferences of the individual magician, and these obviously differ from culture to culture. For example, if you have never before been confronted with Indian bhajans or

Tibetan ritual music, you will probably have trouble falling into any kind of trance and be more preoccupied with thoughts such as "Turn off that awful howling sound!"

The volume of music is a debatable issue that strongly depends on individual listening preferences. Those who have been torturing their eardrums to near deafness for years in clubs and at live concerts will probably want to turn it up full blast. Although I personally believe that a person should (re)learn to listen to more subtle sounds.

According to my humble experience on the subject, pure cacophonies are only, at best, suitable for divination. Since the human brain cannot stand "meaningless" stimuli for a sustained period of time, it will attempt to find patterns in the tonal chaos. If a person is skilled in knowing how to use this, he or she can construct an oracle (a sort of acoustic inkblot test) with the hopes of luring sound-associated answers to arise from the depths of one's own psyche.

By the way, I think it is a bunch of nonsense when those die-hard "New Agers" sometimes claim that modern rock and pop music is detrimental to the organism, the aura, the chakras, the karma, or whatever else. (By the way, that reminds me of the aphorism by

Emil Cioran: "Music is the refuge of souls ulcerated by happiness." How about looking at things this way for a change?!) It may be true that Led Zeppelin and The Cure have no great fans among the plant world (as tests supposedly have proven), but can this be assumed about people, too? If you look at the history of rock 'n' roll, you will see that this type of music had only one goal in mind—to create a state of ecstasy in the listener. And in the end, that is the ultimate goal of any type of music.

That is why a musick magician should try and expand his or her listening experience as much as possible. Just listening to nothing but rock or punk is one-sided and therefore pragmatically useless, especially if the sound of ba-*rock* or *rock*-oco makes you nervous and want to cover your ears (or the other way around, of course).

Merry melodies!
Aunt Klara

How does a death spell work?

Dear Aunt Klara, How does a death spell actually work?

Verena P. from D.

My dear Verena,

That is something you do not ask about in public! What will the neighbors think of us?

But seriously now: there is no such thing as an "ultimate" death spell, and if you are looking for a patented recipe here, I am sorry to disappoint you.

To experts it is no secret that death spells are among the most difficult types of magical undertakings of all. And there is a good reason for that. A death spell is directed at the primeval source of the target person's magical power—namely, that person's survival instinct. There is no better protection than that; after all, this survival instinct makes life as we know it possible in the first place. We can safely do away with the old, pseudo-enlightened claim that death spells only work if the victim is informed about them. That may be a fine, reassuring placebo theory for esoteric softies, but not for grim coffee-sipping aunts like us who meet on a daily basis to pleasurably poke voodoo dolls with our knitting needles.

There are plenty of successful cases in which the victim has absolutely no idea what powers have been released so suddenly and specifically. Of course, I do not want to entirely eliminate the possibility that it sometimes works this way. In fact, it really is often a lot easier for the magician when the target person's beliefs just take care of the rest after a dramatic death announcement is made. And since magicians are notoriously lazy people, they are often satisfied with just that—although the professional skeptics among us will conclude that this is exactly what it's all about.

But now I would like to reveal something to you, my dear evil little Verena (because you obviously have a personal interest in the subject, which the feigned neutral wording of your question reveals): almost all magical attacks are targeted at the victim's immune system. (No, no, no . . . please do not bring AIDS into the picture here. That really has nothing to do with it!) This is quite logical, because once the immune system is weakened, even the smallest, most seemingly harmless bacterium can become a potential ally of the attacker. Magical operations that aim at weakening the victim's aura, spells to cause confusion and disintegration, and of course, the ever-so-popular car-crash magic—all of these techniques are used by magical villains to knock off members of the black list: rich aunts (no, I am not, so don't even try), mothers-in-law, spouses, rivals, bosses, teachers, lawyers, judges, neighbors, and even unloved pets.

But never fear. Only on rare occasions are death spells truly deadly. The victim's inner resistance (the Master Therion might say the person's True Will) is usually much too strong. But there are worse things than death anyway: for example, life as a zombie.

At this point, I need to warn you against the widespread opinion that all "black magic" will automatically bounce back to the initiator sooner or later. Unfortunately—or luckily?—there is no such automatic mechanism, no such cosmic motherly regeneration process. No, there are other ways to protect yourself from a death spell—but that was not what you asked, was it?

So I would like to wrap this up now with sappy, sweet greetings. The best of luck to you—whatever that might mean!

Yours, Aunt Klara

WHAT EXACTLY IS INFORMATION MAGIC?

HAIL, AUNT KLARA, WITH ALL THAT IS SACRED TO YOU! I RECENTLY READ SOMETHING ABOUT INFORMATION MAGIC AND WAS TRULY FASCINATED. CAN YOU EXPLAIN HOW TO STABILIZE A NOTION (OR EVEN MORE) BY MEANS OF THIS SO-CALLED INFORMATION MAGIC? WHAT EXACTLY IS INFORMATION MAGIC ANYWAY? I WILL BE AWAITING YOUR ANSWERS WITH A WIDE GRIN ON MY FACE.

XXV–IV:989

Dear XXV–IV:989!

Wow, that sure is a mouthful of questions. Let me take one at a time.

Information magic—Frater U.·. D.·. calls this discipline "cyber magic" (from *magic* and *cybernetics* = control theory)—is one of the oldest and, at the same time, most modern forms of magic around. So to start with, here is a quick lesson in the history of magic:

Probably the oldest model of magic is the one that works with spirits. Here, a clear distinction is made between the world of humans and the spirit world. The magician acts as an intermediary (or border crosser) between these two worlds, and is able to happily romp around in the spirit realm just as he or she does among humans—and among clients who make use of the magician's services. Such spirits are treated as real beings that actually exist, each having its own name, customs, likes and dislikes, talents, and shortcomings. The magician who works with this model must research the laws of this spirit world and travel to it unless its residents are summoned down to Earth, although that is not really the finest way to do things. One learns the names and secret passwords of the spirits, meanders through their hierarchies, and attempts to gain as many allies and make as few enemies as possible. These spirits will then actively serve the magician and bring about the desired effects on the physical plane.

So far, so good. But as we all know, with this model magic remains stuck in its development, just like the rest of our "highly civilized" human race.

Around the time of the French Revolution, parallel to the trends of enlightenment and rationalism, the field of natural science showed an interest in researching energies. That did not happen overnight, of course, and this phase lasted for a very long time. In fact, it is still ongoing, and one could even go so far as to say that this energy model of magic is popular now in these modern times. If you would like a few names for reference, here is a short list: Franz Anton Mesmer, the rediscoverer of hypnotism and animal magnetism who mesmerized people in salons throughout Europe, putting countless clients and victims into a deep sleep; English Rosicrucian and magician Edward Bulwer-Lytton, who coined the term *vril* to describe magical or subtle energy; Eliphas Lévi, who put into words the theory of "astral light"; Karl von Reichenbach, still highly appreciated today, whose *od* has become a standard term in the occult;

Madame Blavatsky, who liked to steal ideas from others, such as the Indian concept of *prana*; a handful of unnamed ethnologists who first introduced the Polynesian concept of *mana* to academic discussions; and finally Frater U.·. D.·., who sinned in this sense as well by attempting to introduce the word *magis* to mean magical power, although apparently he has not been very successful at it.

But what is the energy model all about? Here we can gladly do without all those spirits, demons, souls from the dead, and similar creatures. Instead, the magician becomes a sort of artist who works with energy. The magician can perceive a whole lot more than just physical energy—after all, anyone can do that. Instead, the magician trains his or her subtle perception, learns to direct subtle energies, to send and withdraw them, and naturally to polarize them as well, or even to "inoculate" them with statements of intent.

Let us take healing as an example. To heal someone, a shamanic spirit magician would try to identify the spirit that haunts the person and expel the monster using all the tricks in the book, including threats and bribery. He or she might also use spirit helpers to heal the sick person. But the energy magician would

go about it quite differently. First, the energy magician would examine the balance of subtle energy in
the patient and determine if there is too much or too
little energy in certain spots. Then the energy balance
would be restored by withdrawing or adding energy
as appropriate, without having to worry about the
various hierarchies of spirits.

Of course, this does not exclude the possibility
of mixed-model forms. The example of Polynesian
mana clearly shows that a magical culture is certainly
able to work with both spirits *and* energies. These
models, therefore, serve more as a means of illustra-
tion, and not every word should be taken literally.
Also, in no way does this mean that one model has
completely edged out and replaced another in its entirety. For example, traditionalistic magicians (e.g.,
who follow the tradition of Bardon) still prefer to
work with spirits and demons even today. Nonetheless, this does not stop them from building up energy—for example, in the making of ritual weapons,
talismans, and the like.

Since the end of the 1960s, a new model of magic
has developed—once again originating in England—
called the psychological model, whose predecessors
can be found in the works of Austin Osman Spare and

even Aleister Crowley. With this model, the power to cause magical phenomena is ascribed to the subconscious mind, and so it is a logical consequence that the psychological magician is mainly concerned with its conditioning. This can be accomplished, for example, through the generous use of magical paraphernalia and external stimuli (incense, robes, colorful sigils, and the whole hodgepodge of magical correspondences). On the other hand, minimalists such as Austin Osman Spare will prefer simple sigils that are quickly made; after all, they are nothing more than commands to the subconscious—or, to put it more technically, intentional repression and the specific creation of complexes.

But before you get a heart attack from all the suspense I am building here, I think it would be time to finally say a few words about information magic itself. On the surface, each of these models seems to be a simplification and reduction of an earlier model. This is extremely obvious when you take a look at cyber magic, since it does not use spirits at all. In cyber magic, energy is no longer a means, but rather it has become the actual goal of the magical operation; and the only purpose that the psyche and subconscious mind have is merely to make decisions on

determining magical targets and to perform the info-
magical operation.

What is the fundamental idea behind this discipline? It is assumed that energy in itself is "dumb."
It needs structure or certain "laws" or "commands"
so that it "knows" how to behave. In a healing operation, the cyber-magician would waste no time at all
with trying to bring spirits, energies, or psychological disturbances under direct control. Instead, he or
she would give the organism of the patient a "healing
input." A sort of "circuit diagram" for health is created within the organism that the energies, psychological structures, and even spirits, if you like, must
adapt to. To illustrate this process, terms from the
field of computer science are used, but it would go
too far here to explain these in detail, especially since
I have no knowledge of your familiarity with comput-
ers, my dear XXV–IV:989.

In any case, this model has considerable advantages.
For one, this type of operation can be performed much
more quickly than other magical techniques. A ritual
using the spirit model may take days, weeks, or even
months. Energy operations that are performed ritually
will take a few hours, whereas a psychological discipline
such as sigil magic can be done in just a few minutes

once a certain degree of proficiency is obtained. On average, the cyber-magical transfer of information takes just a fraction of a second. Plus, no external tools are needed for cyber magic since everything takes place within the participant's own neurocomputer.

According to the current state of knowledge, the prerequisite for successful cyber-magical work is the ability to activate the two main memories of the human organism—the brain and spinal cord. In India, they would call this "awakening the kundalini," but that would take us back to the energy model again.

The whole point is that information in the cyber-magical model does not require a medium (or physical conduit), since information is understood to be non-local and without mass. But since cyber magic is in the developmental stage right now, there is still much to be learned about this aspect. At present, hundreds of magicians around the world are actively experimenting with information magic, and we are curious to see what results they come up with.

But why did I say that this form of magic is probably the oldest? Apart from the fact that a prototype of cyber magic can also be recognized in homeopathy, we are dealing here with a form of the "empty-hand technique," and it is a known fact that such techniques can be found in all magical traditions, at least as an ultimate goal. And who really knows how the Indian rishis or primeval shamanic sorcerers like Odin actually received their knowledge?

Well, I hope I was able to help you. But if you ever ruin a beautiful Sunday of mine again by not letting me attend a publicity event for crocheted potholders, then I will really get mad.

Greetings,
Your Aunt Klara

IS WITCHCRAFT AN ANCIENT EUROPEAN NATURE RELIGION?

DEAREST AUNT KLARA! OVER THE PAST FEW YEARS I HAVE REPEATEDLY COME ACROSS THE TERM "WITCHCRAFT." ONE HEARS AND READS SO MANY DIFFERENT THINGS ABOUT IT, SO TODAY I WOULD LIKE TO ASK YOU WHAT IT IS REALLY ALL ABOUT AND WHAT YOUR OPINION OF IT IS. IS IT REALLY TRUE THAT WITCHCRAFT IS THE ANCIENT EUROPEAN NATURE RELIGION THAT WAS PRACTICED IN THE PRE-CHRISTIAN ERA? I HAVE THE IMPRESSION THAT MANY AUTHORS AND REPRESENTATIVES OF THIS TRADITION LIKE TO USE

THE PAST FOR PROJECTING THEIR OWN FEARS, IMPOSSIBLE DREAMS, AND PROMISING DESIRES.

WALTER Z. FROM F.

Dear Walter,

You probably want me to contradict you, but I am afraid you are entirely correct with your assumptions. All the garbage that is now associated with the once-honest trade of witchcraft is utterly confusing, resulting in the fact that one can hardly tell the difference anymore. This is added to the fact that witchcraft is often misused as a vehicle for transporting foreign ideologies that actually have nothing to do with the Craft itself.

Since the feminist movement has taken over the tradition of witchcraft, the image of the witch in Western civilization has changed dramatically. That is not necessarily bad in principle: men have had time enough to prove what they can and cannot do, and even if this does not make women as a whole more perfect as a result, the role of a witch is a suitable label of identification. After all, it is no secret that in the five hundred years of witch hysteria initiated and controlled by the church, 80 percent of those persecuted were women and not men. However, the fact that it was not only men who staged this persecution but also countless women (and they did so vehemently at that) is usually kept quiet.

But what does this story of misery and human brainlessness actually have to do with the tradition of witchcraft as we know it? Maybe we should take a more systematic approach. So watch out now, dear Walter Z.: Aunt Klara is going to spit out a jumble of historical facts and figures here.

First, we need to establish the fact that there is evidence of the practice of witchcraft throughout the entire world during all eras. But this does not automatically mean that what we are dealing with today (especially in Europe) fulfills the definition of a genuine, centuries-old tradition consisting of an organization of like-minded people that is divided up into a hierarchy and led with a certain amount of authority. Although the respected British Egyptologist Margaret Murray made many such claims, the narrow-minded academic world cannot be made entirely to blame for the fact that her statements contained no more truth than the weather forecasts on television. But to be fair, many of the things Murray claimed can indeed be backed by some facts. On the other hand, however, there is way too little evidence to give her hypothesis about witchcraft being the ancient European nature religion more than a mere shaky status.

What we know today as Wicca developed after World War II when British occultist (and eccentric) Gerald Brosseau Gardner had the audacity to publicly profess his practice of witchcraft and to recruit new members, all despite the British Witchcraft Act. It is no surprise to hear that Gardner was a fan of Margaret Murray and readily adopted her statements as his own. But in spite of this, he did make a few of his own contributions: while his novel *High Magic's Aid* contained mainly dark whisperings and vague insinuations (which, of course, greatly aroused public interest), he was able to really let his pants down a few years later, after the Witchcraft Act was finally abolished. Gardner pole-vaulted himself straight to the top, declaring himself to be an agent of witchcraft who was granted permission—from other, older members of the tradition—to initiate new members. But since these alleged older members remained behind the scenes, as invisible as the "Secret Chiefs" of the Golden Dawn and the Mahatmas of Theosophy, Gardner himself became the head of the Wicca movement.

Modern-day Wicca is a mere sixty years old—quite young if you think about the claims to historical legitimacy that it makes. The assertion that Wicca supposedly had various predecessors cannot change this fact. Admittedly, Charles Godfrey Leland's *Aradia, or the Gospel of the Witches* was published in the late 1800s; and a few years before that, in his book *The Synagogue of Satan*, Stanislaw Przybyszewski posited the existence of a witchcraft tradition in medieval Europe. And more recent research has shown that ancient paganism (which was and still is quite often wrongly confused with witchcraft) was in no way stomped out entirely by Christian missionaries during their crusade of compulsory conversion. Nonetheless, the sad fact remains for the esoteric historian that what is understood today as Wicca, or the tradition called witchcraft, is mainly a romantic conglomeration of predominantly anti-Christian ideals and resentment.

As far as the rest goes, I am probably not the right person to talk to, my dear. Not because I am principally against witches, but rather because I have dedicated my life to the Black Arts and prefer to stay far away from any type of pure religion. Which is basically what Wicca is today. One could describe it in an unfriendly way as a neo-primitive fertility religion that plays merely a subordinate role in magic, at least in its practical application.

To be sure, many covens do their share of conjuring and sorcery, but the fundamental idea remains a religious one. Key phrases such as *Mother Nature, back to the Great Mother, living in harmony with nature,* and the like make this unmistakably clear. That is why I prefer to not make any judgmental calls here. There are some magicians and sorcerers who place great value on the pursuit of some kind of transcendence, regardless of how this may be defined; yet others describe themselves as pure magic technicians who are only concerned with expanding their control over what is known as "fate." Who is to be the judge?

Greetings tainted with panic-stricken laughter . . .

Yours, Aunt Klara

Is there a form of Freemasonry that is magically active?

Dear Aunt Klara, Could you please tell me if there is a form of Freemasonry today that is magically active? I would also appreciate it if you could provide me with a contact address.

Bartholomew M. from D.

My dear Bartholomew,

First of all, I must kindly refuse your request to provide you with an address. There are several reasons for that, including the fact that there really is no current form of Freemasonry that works with magic. Apart from that, it is not my job to provide any type of contact information, which has nothing to do with me trying to be unfriendly, but rather with the fact that magic has always had a bad reputation in the press and those active in this field need to exercise an extreme amount of discretion.

But back to your original question. Many magical orders emerged from exactly this dilemma: that although Freemasonry is a legitimate keeper and preserver of Western magical symbolism and mythology, it has developed into a mere social club with ritualistic and mythical trimmings, to put it nicely. Even today, no one really knows what existed first—Rosicrucianism or Freemasonry. However, one thing is for sure: Rosicrucianism in the nineteenth century held an openly critical opinion of the lack of magical practice within Freemason lodges. This was not enough, though, for contemporaries such as Eliphas Lévi and S. L. "MacGregor" Mathers; thus, various magical lodges and orders were created that did indeed, like it or not, contain elements of Freemasonry, but considered themselves above all to be practical executioners of the "old knowledge" that Freemasonry allegedly was preserving.

But now Freemasonry is a huge movement, and it would surely be unfair to lump all of its various lodges together. As is so often the case, we need to differentiate here between official doctrine and private practice. The official representatives of Freemasonry will usually get quite pale in the face if you link them in any way to esotericism or—*horribile dictu*—magic. Once when I tried asking a Belgian Freemason about his relationship to mysticism, all of a sudden the guy had no idea what I was talking about! It was utterly incomprehensible to him that I could see a connection between Freemasonry and mysticism or the pursuit of transcendence. Well, the guy belonged to the obedience of the Grand Orient of Paris, which is known for having a strong atheistic attitude. But it is not much different with the "Ancient Scots." There you at least have to believe in God, although that certainly does not make it magical.

On the other hand, I know many Freemasons who have made the conscious choice to be magicians as well, and I know for example that Freemasonry in Austria is beginning to sow its first esoteric or magical seeds, which is no wonder considering the growing interest that younger members are showing in such things. However, I am not aware of any (regular) lodge that does any kind of magical work in the least. So whoever is blinded by the nimbus of the ancient venerableness that Freemasonry undoubtedly has, in the attempt to find any kind of knowledge of practical magic there, the search will be in vain. Of course, there is always the chance that you might run into a certain FM brother who is interested in such things, but you probably shouldn't tell the world about it, since the high-ranking leaders will most likely not approve.

It is a bit different in so-called "irregular" Freemasonry, however. Above all, the Rite of Memphis-Misraim should be mentioned here, of which even Aleister Crowley was a member. But I cannot really say for sure whether or not there is really more action there than in other Masonic lodges.

In any case, what we consider to be "magical work" is merely a matter of definition anyway, and varies according to individual conceptions and expectations. While one person might get all weak in the knees just by lighting a candle and muttering the mantra *Om*, another person might be bored at a Black Mass and yearn for some stronger stuff. Ceremonies alone do not make something magic. Surely the average Freemason experiences a number of rituals throughout his life that would make the more sensitive among us tremble in our boots; however, these are not done specifically to influence the way of things, but rather at most to create or open up certain states of consciousness and levels of development. There may be a few souls out there who truly appreciate such things. But beyond that, Freemasonry is hardly more than what its magical critics accuse it of being.

Even if my answer may be a bit frustrating to you, I hope I was able to help you nonetheless. I will keep swinging my trowel for you . . .

Your Aunt Klara

How significant was the Golden Dawn?

Dear Aunt Klara, Over the last few years there has been a big fuss about the Golden Dawn again. Was this order really so significant? I think that most of the information that is available about their teachings is quite old-fashioned, overly complicated, and dogmatic. Or do you feel otherwise?

Simon F. from T.

Dear Simon,

In answer to your question as to whether the Golden Dawn really was so significant, there is only one simple answer: *yes, yes, yes!* No doubt you are familiar with the Lesser Banishing Ritual of the Pentagram. And you have probably heard of the four elemental weapons of magic—the chalice, sword, wand, and pentacle. Those are just two examples of the great influence that the Golden Dawn has had on contemporary magic. But there is a whole lot more. Although I hear again and again from people who seem to think that the Pentagram Ritual is as old as time itself, I unfortunately have to disappoint them. This ritual as we know it today was developed by the Golden Dawn. And before this order existed, no one even knew that the four suits of the Minor Arcana could also be used in practical ritual magic. This, too, was an invention of the Golden Dawn.

Yet I am not saying that this order did not fall back on older sources, too. In fact, its main contribution consists of exactly that—the members of the Golden Dawn collected material from a variety of different disciplines and combined it. The leading figure behind all of this was Samuel Liddell "MacGregor"

Mathers, founder and later sole leader of the order. He was a colorful and eccentric character, surely one of the most significant self-taught magicians of his time, though also one of the greatest megalomaniacs. In my opinion, his achievements are equal to those of Agrippa.

In this sense, I need to correct you in your comment about the Golden Dawn supposedly being dogmatic and antiquated. Admittedly, when we page through some of the documents today, much of the material seems hopelessly outdated and may even turn us off. How many modern magicians like rituals with antiquated Anglican Church English that take hours to perform and deliver at best only meager results? And the constant secrecy can really get on your nerves after a while. But it would be wrong to throw out the child along with the bathwater and measure everything according to the standards of current times. I would even go so far as to say that the mere fact that you are interested in magic at all stems back to the groundwork once laid by the Golden Dawn.

Now let us take a brief look at the magical situation in the 1800s. That was a time when the hardliners of the rational sciences boldly claimed to have finally bumped off religion and all other forms of so-called irrationalism once and for all. Some thought it would be just a matter of a few decades or one or two generations before the "opiate of the people" would have worn itself out. The world is a clockwork—that was the motto of this era. The enormous progress that had been made in sciences such as physics, chemistry, medicine, and even engineering all contributed to the idealization of this motto. Occultism was entirely on the defensive. What was once knowledge that was reserved exclusively for the ruling class was suddenly degraded to the "metaphysics of stupid guys" (Adorno). The ultimate explanation of the world seemed just moments away from discovery. Occultism was out, and magic was considered to be utterly impossible. Nonetheless, Francis Barrett published his work *The Magus* in 1801, and even if people are still talking about it today, it was little more than a collection of late medieval hocus-pocus, and quite incomplete at that.

Of course, there were counter-movements as well. We can safely forget about the religious revivalist movement that flared up all over the world back then, regardless of the fact that occultists later recruited members from this scene, just as they do today as well. Rosicrucianism was more significant, however, especially in England and France, for producing such illustrated figures as Bulwer-Lytton and paving the way for the Golden Dawn. Preliminary work was done above all by Eliphas Lévi, who put forth great efforts to make magic intellectually acceptable again, and his student and/or successor Papus, who successfully advanced to the position of occult advisor to Czar Nicholas II's court. There was bustling activity among the Parisian bohemians as well, with figures such as Stanislas de Guaita and Joséphin Péladan stirring up quite a storm. But it was Mathers who knew how to interpret the signs of the time by founding the Golden Dawn, thus presenting a system that was complicated and comprehensive enough to meet the high expectations of erudite intellectuals who were sick and tired of Manchester industrialism and were on the lookout for a new spiritual home.

Influences of the Golden Dawn can be recognized in every documented form of Western magic from the 1900s onward. As Papus discovered the Jewish Kabbalah for the tarot while indulging endlessly in highly complicated gematric and numerological speculations, Mathers complemented this with his concept of astral travel ("rising up through the levels") and practical Kabbalistic pathworking, thus creating a comprehendible form of practice. While the teachings of the Indian tattwas remained purely theoretical in Theosophy, the Golden Dawn used this concept for its astral travels. Although a clear distinction has been made since ancient times between the functions of an amulet and those of a talisman, and although there is early evidence of planetary magic being practiced as well, it was the Golden Dawn that understood how to turn it into a coherent system with fundamental principles that still apply today.

Mathers studied massive amounts of old material, adapting it to fit the times he lived in and adding his own ideas. However, the result was not what we know as ancient hermetic magic, but rather a variation of it à la the Golden Dawn. English and German authors kept rehashing the Golden Dawn system from the mid-1800s onward, with its climax in the 1970s and 1980s, and although the wave of German occultism remained independent of the Golden Dawn at first, such literature later influenced it much more than anything else.

You might shrug this off as a purely historical phenomenon, but then please tell me how you would go about studying Enochian magic without drawing from the sources of the Golden Dawn?

One helpful hint: try to not let the old-fashioned style of the Golden Dawn bother you so much, and focus instead on recognizing the basic structures that are relevant to your own personal practice. Surely you can find the essential practical material of the Golden Dawn system in literature by other authors where it is explained much more precisely and understandably. Nonetheless, I recommend that every magician who takes his or her art and science seriously personally study such pertinent original sources. Of course, you will not be interested in doing this if you are only interested in practice and not in theory and fundamental research. But if that is the case, then please do not complain when you have to rediscover the wheel over and over again just because you did not do your homework.

Magical development also means slowly separating yourself from your own predecessors. However, after the unavoidable phase of revolutionary iconoclasm, it would be foolish to cling to adolescent obstinacy instead of expressing a more objective and rational form of appreciation and criticism.

In this sense, I hope you will be able to replace the Golden Dawn system with your own techniques real soon!

Yours, Aunt Klara

Do "true" Satanists really exist?

Aunt Klara, help! No matter what newspaper I open up, or what magazine I page through, everywhere I see headlines such as "Juveniles in the claws of Satanists," "Satanic cults in schools," and "Black Mass held during lunch break." I have the vague feeling that such scandal-mongering journalism is throwing a whole bunch of different things together into one pot. Is there really such a thing as Satanists anyway? Can you help?

ELFRIEDE H. FROM B.

Dear Elfriede,

Sigh, that's what I was afraid of! Well, well, my dear, many a poor old witch has asked this question herself: is there even such a thing as Satanism? But first a few words about the current media hype. It certainly is possible that séances are sometimes held at schools, with table-rapping, automatic writing, and other types of spirit conjuration, but most incidents are probably meant more as a joke. Of course, sensationalist journalism loves things like that and publishes them big. Then dear little children everywhere are approached by their parents about these horrible fairy tales ("Do you have things like that at your school, too, dear?") and think to themselves, "That's an awesome idea! We should try that out!"

Do not accuse me of playing the situation down, though. After all, the theory that so-called "juvenile Satanism" is being systematically hyped by the media was recently confirmed to me by a religious-cult advisor who, by the way, takes the whole thing a lot less seriously than a vehement atheist of a more rationalistic nature might do.

But in reality, dear Elfriede, you are actually looking for "true," "genuine" Satanists who have truly earned their reputation, right? This boils down to a problem of definition, though. Because what one person defines as Satanism, another might call spiritual Christianity. In this sense, extremists in the church hierarchy have sometimes gone so far as to claim that Transcendental Meditation is Satanic, and some Christian fundamentalists think that everything that lies outside the vision field of their pious blinders is the devil's work. And wasn't the image of the devil invented by the church hierarchy in the first place? Oh, how wistful my little sorceress heart becomes when I think about what they did to our good ole Pan! And how they had to erect their chapels and cathedrals right on top of the sites that were previously used by other "devilish" cults to perform their "dirty little deeds." One can never please such simple souls, and if you want to define Satanism like that, then there are of course plenty of Satanists out there.

But how do those people who consider themselves to be true Satanists view this? Well, since you don't run into them every afternoon at your favorite café, we are forced to fall back on the various forms of literature. Satanism is often defined as a form of reversed Catholicism. And indeed this may have applied for the most part to salon Satanists of the late nineteenth century.

Inversion is a typical characteristic of this, known back then as a "reversal of values," which Nietzsche popularized into a mega cultural topic. But this is always defined through a love-hate relationship with the dreadful model of the Catholic Church. For example, the notorious Black Mass is usually nothing more than the inversion of the Catholic High Mass. Whether the Our Father is said backwards (although I have never run into anyone who has seriously practiced such a perfect example of this nonsense), whether crosses are worn upside down, or whether the Holy Communion is desecrated by substituting it with excrement or urine—each of these would be impossible without immediate references being made to the Catholic Church. This includes the common belief in many so-called "Satanic" circles that, in order for it to be effective, the Black Mass may only be performed by a former Catholic priest who turned disloyal or was suspended.

With the key word *inversion*, we have already identified the basic principle of Satanism fairly well. After all, there is a good reason why Satan is known as "the spirit that ever denies." In this sense, he is the necessary complement to or antagonist of the good God of creation that we are familiar with in a deistic or monotheistic world view. Wasn't it Lucifer who once proclaimed, *"Non serviam!"*?

Pete Carroll and Frater U∴ D∴ have often pointed out that a Black Mass held in modern times should actually contain entirely different elements instead of just trying to break down ancient, crumbling doors that have already been wide open for a good hundred years in the first place. In this sense, magicians described as Satanists should be less concerned with turning Christian symbols of martyrdom upside down and more concerned with slamming a brick into the television set during the international soccer finals. They should recite stock market prices and weather forecasts backwards instead of attacking the Bible, which they probably know virtually nothing about anyway. What I just said about the Black Mass applies, of course, *mutatis mutandis*, to Satanism as a whole.

But the true magician wants a whole lot more. Since his or her real concern is always just magic and power, which can be more loosely defined as "efficiency," the magician is never satisfied with confirming the existing world order by provoking it. That only causes a stalemate instead of dissolving something, as every revolution has always proved over and over again. But when the spirit of opposition is taken one step further, its tender roots will soon wrap around solid rocks. Then the magician is no longer satisfied with things such as gravity or the complicated process of metabolism. Not that these and other such things have already been mastered, but at least one never stops trying to do so. In this sense, the magician can never really be anything other than a "Satanist" if he or she accordingly wants to assume sole control of his or her life and what we refer to as destiny. The fact that this has nothing at all to do with the Satanism that we hear about in the media should be obvious. In the same way, such Satanists also have nothing at all to do with magic; after all, their persistent hate and rejection of orthodox systems only serves in making these systems even more powerful, thus achieving just the opposite of their original intentions.

> With jet-black greetings,
> Your Aunt Klara

WHAT IS THE TRUTH BEHIND SIGIL MAGIC?

DEAR AUNT KLARA! LATELY THERE HAVE BEEN ARTICLES EVEN IN CONVENTIONAL MAGAZINES ABOUT SIGIL MAGIC. PLUS, THERE ARE LOTS OF BOOKS AVAILABLE ON THE SUBJECT TODAY: FOR EXAMPLE, A HANDBOOK BY FRATER U∴ D∴. NOW, SIGIL MAGIC IS SUPPOSEDLY SO PLAIN AND SIMPLE—SO SIMPLE, IN FACT, THAT THE BASICS COULD EASILY BE EXPLAINED ON A SINGLE SHEET OF PAPER. WHY THE FLOOD OF PUBLICATIONS THEN? IS IT ALL JUST A MONEY-MAKING SCAM, OR IS THERE MORE TO SIGIL MAGIC THAN MEETS THE EYE?

PETER D. FROM H.

My dear Peter,

To say "lots of books" is a bit of an exaggeration, especially in comparison to the number of books available on other subjects, such as protective magic, healing techniques, or the making of talismans.

But generally speaking, you are quite correct. Sigil magic is so plain and simple that the basic principles really can be summarized in just a few words: write down your statement of intent, create a graphic sign from the letters after crossing out those that are repeated, and charge it spasmodically in a state of trance—that is the simple formula for sigil magic. Oh, and don't forget to forget about it!

But that is the snag to the whole thing. Generally, a successful magical operation does not even require such a "complicated" procedure as making a sigil. One of the many empty-handed techniques is "quick thinking," in which a thought is briefly formulated but not pursued any further, and then immediately forgotten. I am sure you are familiar with this from everyday life situations, and that such situations usually turn out negatively—for example, when you park in a no-parking zone, get out of the car, and think for a split second, "I hope I don't get a ticket." But of course, when you return to the car there is a ticket under the windshield wipers.

Magical disciplines such as "positive thinking" have disguised the actual problem a bit by claiming that the negative nature of such thoughts is the only reason that they are manifested. But the same thing can happen with positive thoughts, too. For example, you think briefly about a friend and express the desire, "I hope he calls me soon"—and then the phone rings. Of course, it will often be exactly that friend, even if you haven't heard from him in years. But we could explain such things as simple "divination" or "telepathy," too. Indeed this brings up the further question as to whether many so-called magical acts are possibly nothing more than an expression or manifestation of telepathically received impulses. In other words, you might sense that your friend wants to call you and formulate this feeling into a desire. Neither theory can be proved, though, at least not in a scientific sense, since we simply do not know enough about the truly relevant factors.

What I am trying to make clear with this little excursus is that even in sigil magic, the last word has definitely not been spoken yet. After all (cross your heart), as everyone knows, creating the sigil itself is the least of our problems. More often than not, the real problem is truly forgetting about the whole operation. In addition, every sigil magician realizes sooner or later that he or she automatically develops his or her own techniques, thus eventually creating one's own personal form of sigil magic. That should clear up the question as to why so much can be written about such a seemingly simple discipline.

Often we forget that sigil magic is an integral part of the magical system from Austin Osman Spare, who liked to decorate his own pictures and graphics with sigils. Austin Osman Spare created a self-sufficient "alphabet of desire," introduced the shamanic principle of working with atavisms to Western magic (again), systematically expanded on the Freudian concept of repression for magical purposes (thus the significance of forgetting), and made numerous other contributions to magic, making him all the more fascinating.

Every sigil-magical operation touches on the question of the immanent effectiveness of magical symbols. In more dogmatic types of magic, it was previously commonplace to assume that certain objectively effective protection symbols should be used, such as the pentagram, cross, hexagram, circle, and so on. Both psychological and pragmatic forms of magic have challenged this dogma, however, with their practitioners insisting that a symbol cannot become effective until it is programmed into the magician's subconscious. In my opinion, this is true, based on the practical results of my own work with protection symbols.

Maybe you'd like to work with sigils yourself for a while so you can contribute your own ideas to the conversation. That would make an old lady very happy!

Your Aunt Klara

What truth is there to all the rumors about the Fraternitas Saturni?

Dear Aunt Klara! I've read a lot about the Fraternitas Saturni in older publications, and unfortunately not all of it has been good. There are lots of rumors floating around. For example, the order was supposedly dissolved in the 1970s. And allegedly there are several orders operating under the same name. Some people claim that the older members of the brotherhood use the order as a mere reservoir for "fresh

**OD" AND THAT THEY FEED OFF THE NEWER MEM-
BERS LIKE VAMPIRES. I THINK THIS ALL SOUNDS
PRETTY OUTRAGEOUS, SO I THOUGHT I WOULD
ASK IF YOU HAVE ANY MORE INFORMATION ON
THE SUBJECT.**

SABINE F. FROM C.

Dear Sabine,

Yes, there are a lot of rumors out there about the Fraternitas Saturni, and *outrageous* certainly is a good word
to describe them. Of course, the order is not entirely
innocent in this matter. In the 1960s in particular it was
surrounded by a great deal of controversy. During this
period, there was lots of nitpicking and pedantry of a
type more characteristic to a group of rabbit breeders,
and someone was constantly being excommunicated.
That absorbed most of the members' energy, and nothing truly innovative for modern magic resulted from
this period.

The fluctuation of members was always quite high,
even stemming back to the early days when the order
was founded by Gregor A. Gregorius, as can be read
in the official announcements in the publication *Blät-
ter für angewandte okkulte Lebenskunst* (Journal for Applied Occult Life Mastery). In some years, fluctuation

was even as high as 50 percent, and the fact that the FS (as we'll refer to it) had over a hundred members at times did not help—although this is a pretty high number for any German order! In any case, the order had masters and even grandmasters who mercilessly sold off parts of the internal archives, or let themselves be tricked by equally conniving archive hunters and occult bibliomaniacs who robbed them of the treasures that they were entrusted with. Plus, schisms (end even split-off organizations) were commonplace, as were legal quarrels and dogmatic appeals; in fact, the systematic persecution of dissentious outsiders was a major factor that contributed to the FS's reputation, which follows it even today.

But back to your questions. Yes, I can tell you a bit about the FS, but please do not ask me to reveal my source of information (which I can assure you is highly reliable).

Following its reestablishment at the end of World War II, the order has existed continually since then as a legally registered society. (The FS was banned during the Nazi regime, as were all occult organizations. In fact, Gregorius himself was persecuted. He fled to Italy but was handed back over to Germany by Mussolini's regime and ended up in "preventive detention" for roughly one year.) Contradictory claims of certain schisms had only one goal in mind—to be able to decorate their own secret organizations with the fascinating name *Fraternitas Saturni*. This is a legally established fact, because in the early 1980s a further split-off occurred, and a new organization began to call itself "Fraternitas Saturni" until a court order required them to stop.

The Fraternitas Saturni follows the same clever policy as the Vatican—namely, to neither publicly confirm nor deny anything at all. In the same way, the order (which is a legal entity) took no legal action against Werner Schmitz when he presented them as little more than a pornography and blackmail undertaking in his novel *Auf Teufel komm raus*. The dignified behavior on the part of the order was surely a clever move, since denial and legal action would only provide fuel for the fire. By ignoring the claims, they naturally faded from the public eye.

The headquarters of the "lodge" (as the group calls itself) is located in Berlin again, and not in the Frankfurt region as it was for many years in the past.

The FS has undergone a thorough transformation over the last few decades. The average age of the members has drastically dropped, which naturally has an effect on the group's practical work. A merger with another magical order has taken place as well, which expanded membership and added even more young members.

Principally, the FS does not canvass for new members—not because they are trying to hide something, but rather because they hold the opinion that everyone who is supposed to find their way to the order will do so eventually on his or her own. Besides, from what I hear, they place a lot more value on quality than on quantity. The practical training that a neophyte receives is much more rigorous than it was in the past, and since capacities are limited as far as qualified trainers go, they are not interested in initiating more people than they can take care of.

I am not familiar enough with the order's history to exclude the possibility that vampirism might have once been practiced. If you look at the style of what Michael D. Eschner described as "old-man occultism of the 1920s," this accusation might not be all that far-fetched. But my personal respect for the old men in the FS is not sufficient enough to deem them truly capable of such feats.

It is much more likely that this is all just a misunderstanding, something that probably affects all traditional orders, and not just the FS. In line with the spirit model of magic, every organization creates its own "group spirit," which can also be called an "egregore." However, the FS is one of the very few groups that has actually integrated this fact systematically into its grade system and training plan. Practical work with the egregore is one of the central themes in the order today, which in turn brings us back to the allegations of vampirism. After all, an egregore is nothing but an entity created more or less artificially and intentionally from group energies. Such an entity lives off of this energy, which can be applied in the interest of the group, whether for protection from prosecution or for other common goals. With the wink of an eye, this might be called "vampirism," because an egregore—and this cannot be stressed enough—is not a protective spirit that is appointed to an organization by some higher authority. Instead, it is more of a collective product that is created by the group itself, but one that also has a certain degree of autonomy. So it is only logical that all members of the group are "tapped into" by this entity, whether they realize it or not.

You can probably tell what I am getting at here, but in any case, I am not trying to de-demonize the term *vampirism*. In the same way, you could claim with the same legitimacy that a talisman you charged is vampirizing you as long as you allow it to be effective. Or you might call the treasurer of any organization a "vampire," as some people like to do (ha ha!).

However, if you take a look at the careers of some of the old masters of the FS, you will not get the impression that they could have accomplished great things as vampires. On the contrary, every grandmaster of the order to this day has endured the severity of the Saturnian current to its fullest—and that is what the FS focuses on in the first place. So it would be more accurate to say that all members feed the egregore and the job of the masters is, at most, to work with this entity on a magical-ceremonial level in the group's interest, to "handle" it in a sense and to use it for the lodge.

Of course, a handful of young occultists still think of the FS as a collection of lascivious, drooling old men who stretch their long, sticky fingers out to grope at the legs of sexy young initiates. But I am afraid that anyone who tries to contact the lodge for exactly this reason will be bitterly disappointed.

Whoever wants to become a member of the FS today is subject to a rigorous selection procedure that stretches over a fairly long period of time. The selection is narrowed down already during the early stages, and even if a candidate receives a positive response following an interview, it usually takes at least a year before the candidate is finally initiated into the lodge. While many other orders follow the old German government policy of "time will sort things out, and the more time the better," and award grades and degrees by mail, the earned degrees in the FS actually have to be *earned*—just like in the O.T.O. On another note, a few years ago the FS launched a financial tour de force and succeeded in buying back a large portion of its former possessions. In my opinion, these are all indicators that we are no longer dealing with a weak organization whose members are fighting amongst themselves, as the rumors might indicate.

Most orders have their ups and downs, and the FS is certainly no exception. The only ones who will have a problem with this, though, are those who still think that magicians are better than other people. But that is a statement we want nothing to do with!

Yours, Aunt Klara

How important was the German magic scene in the 1920s?

Dear Aunt Klara! You often hear about significant figures in the German magic scene in the 1920s: Musallam, Quintscher, Gregorius, and Sebottendorff, just to mention a few, along with a few earlier ones like Staudenmaier. How do you rate the influence of this period, in particular the contribution of German occultism to modern-day magic? Do these magicians still have any relevance today? Is it worthwhile to

STUDY THEM, OR DO YOU THINK IT IS JUST A WASTE OF TIME?

KARL-HEINZ T. FROM F.

Dear Karl-Heinz,

As usual, I prefer to address your question by rambling on like a typical old auntie and will avoid individually judging each of the magicians you've mentioned (and there are a whole lot more who could fall into this category as well). I don't think that would be a very good idea anyway, since it would most likely be far off the mark of what you actually want to know.

It is common for every new generation to feel much more clever and advanced than the one before it. This is merely a reflection of the individual's development in breaking away from the parents and family in social terms. After all, the generational conflict takes place outside the home as well. Plus, it is always difficult to judge a past era when not much time has elapsed since its end. The process of breaking away, which can often lead to an outright revolution, is too fresh in our memories, and thus we can often observe how the grandchildren take over the positions of their grandparents without necessarily being reactionary themselves, while nonetheless preferring to have their tongues torn out than admitting in the slightest that their parents might have actually been right about one thing or another. Although this is nothing new, we have to keep an eye on it if we want to observe a certain period from a neutral point of view. Magic is no exception in this sense, even if I have to regretfully admit that most magicians fail to recognize this historical awareness. Some even go a bit too far and rob themselves of the valuable experience of applying the law of constant change (that they are so fond of quoting) to everything imaginable except to the history of magic itself.

Concerning the specific era that you mentioned, please do not expect me to be entirely neutral in my opinion; after all, this period was way too diversified and much too recent to view with an objective eye. So we can only operate with approximations here.

For now, I would like to diverge a bit and take a look at magic in the 1920s in conjunction with the Black Arts at the end of the nineteenth century and the turn of the twentieth century. After all, many of the things that began to blossom in the 1920s, but also later, in the 1960s and 1970s, had already taken root back in the nineteenth century.

Geographical displacement should be taken into consideration here as well. While Germany was considered to be the stronghold of the magical arts during the late seventeenth and early eighteenth centuries (just think of the Rosicrucians and the hysteria concerning the Illuminates of that period), the focus clearly shifted to France and England around the time of the French Revolution. Without exaggeration, we can safely say that the impulse triggered by the Rosicrucians set the pace for all of European occultism during the early nineteenth century. Authors such as Lévi and Papus placed more emphasis, however, on Jewish and Kabbalistic influences, while Blavatsky initially delved into ancient Egypt before making a sudden turn by introducing ancient knowledge from India into Western occultism. In the 1860s, the Fox sisters in the United States triggered an international wave of spiritualism that determined the course for a large part of the magic scene (at least in the English-speaking world) that lasted well into the 1920s.

Since the Golden Dawn originally developed from a Rosicrucian group called the *Societas Rosicruciana in Anglia* (SRIA), it was consequentially largely influenced by Rosicrucian elements. Although the founding members of the Golden Dawn were all high-ranking

Freemasons, the influence of Freemasonry was limited to the use of Masonic symbolism.

Generally speaking, the situation was a bit different in Germany. Of course, there was a bit of proliferation here and there. Particularly mentionable in this context is Staudenmaier, whom you alluded to in your question. His book *Die Magie als experimentelle Naturwissenschaft* (Magic as an Experimental Science) is, in my opinion, highly overestimated and basically a study of self-induced obsession that has actually very little to do with active magic, but bows to coincidence and fate instead. On the other hand, German/Polish occultist and writer Przybyszewski belongs to the group of unbridled tempers. He took up the act as salon Satanist, admired pseudo-Rosicrucians such as Péladan, Stanislas de Guaita, and other French occultists, but also wrote about witchcraft and never let himself be pushed into one specific direction. And he never contributed anything unique to the occult practice. In this sense, he and his kind could probably be considered among the vast number of "simple-minded" occultists.

Generally, though, the German occultist felt more obligated to the Masonic tradition than to the Rosicrucian one, even if this took the form of actually opposing it. In my opinion, Theodor Reuss and his O.T.O. were always appropriately categorized as quasi-Masonic, and no secret is made about the fact that Aleister Crowley had a soft spot for the Rite of Memphis-Misraim. It is not really important whether or not the individual representatives of German occultism in the 1920s actually were Freemasons themselves or how they might have felt about Freemasonry. Many Masonic elements are clearly present anyway, such as the ritual structure in the Fraternitas Saturni—which, after all, has been one of the leading magical organizations in the German-speaking world since 1928.

On the other hand, I do not want to give the impression here that everything was predominantly Masonic. Much more important is the fact that, although all of German occultism was headed in one specific direction—if we can speak at all of one single homogenous direction in the first place—it was greatly influenced by strong individual personalities and remained rooted in the visions and charisma of these individuals. In the end, religion was always more important to them than magic. Musallam wanted to create a world religion with his Adonism, and Quintscher clung long enough to his coattails while never really giving up this endeavor; Tränker and the Pansophic movement also pursued plans for saving the world, just like Freemasonry and Rosicrucianism have always done. In this sense, Quintscher's pupil Bardon—who first began publishing his own books in the 1950s—was a most welcomed change of pace!

But you asked about the impact that German magic of the 1920s has on the magic of today. Concerning the practical aspect of magic, I don't think it has had much significance at all. The magical techniques documented from that era consist of relatively primitive yoga elements combined with mild imagination exercises and a flood of dogmatic instructions, nearly all of which were copied from Paracelsus and Agrippa. Pansexuality, which was officially only practiced in the O.T.O., had a relatively strong influence, and traces of it can be found in many other groups. One could almost say that the German magicians of this era were "obsessed" by women. But with this attitude, they were merely reflecting the spirit of the times, because this subject dominated European culture as a whole from the mid-nineteenth century through roughly the end of the 1920s; at the same time, the figure of Pan was predominant as an icon of vitality and sexual liberation.

One thing is certain: Quintscher and Bardon re-defined the magical arts, thus establishing new standards that we simply cannot ignore. But the example that I often like to use of magicians acquiring mediums trained to obey them is also a common example of the style of this entire period. However, it would be wrong to leave it at that with such a bitter analysis, since it sounds like I am just picking on people who are no longer around to defend themselves.

In any case, we can surely learn something from the occultism of the 1920s: namely, the ruthless determination in one's own magical operations. If we read the letters that Quintscher wrote to Silas, we may not be particularly impressed by Quintscher's skills—but then again, the same applies to Crowley's diaries. The more decisive factor here, in my opinion, is that these magicians understood how to integrate the Black Arts into their lives in such a comprehensive way, one that could easily be described as "holistic" without overexaggerating. Surely you are aware of my opinion that the persecution of the Inquisition has never really ended. But it is an entirely different story today when we claim to be initiates of the magical arts during times of relative material stability as compared to the times of Crowley, Quintscher, Gregorius, and

Bardon, who were condemned, persecuted, and at times even subjected to physical or mental violence. Just the mere fact that they stuck to their guns under such adverse conditions is certainly worth shedding a tear for, and even if we may not think the world of these people's magical contributions, we should treat them with deserved respect and at least regard them as exemplary ancestors due to their determination and integrity.

As far as the practical impact of occultism in the 1920s, I have already hinted at the fact that its accomplishments were not all that impressive, except for maybe Quintscher's notorious Tepa or his invention of battery magic. (Obviously I will not mention non-German authors here, such as Aleister Crowley and Austin Osman Spare.) When reading books from this era, one thing I notice time and again is how much effort was put into getting just the tiniest results and how such magicians felt compelled to judge human nature, as when Gregorius or Bardon endeavor to criticize civilization itself, or how magicians like Tränker & Co. feel the need with all naïve sincerity to (inaccurately) predict the development of humanity over the next forty years. Certainly you might find a valuable tidbit of practical information here and there, but is it really worth all the effort? I would say yes, although for entirely different reasons than you might expect.

It is also possible to learn from a bad example, so if we really want to know how *not* to do it, the documented history of the orders of this era are the perfect subjects of study. As already mentioned, in the interest of a precise historic overview a person could study this era endlessly. However, the practical magic of contemporary magicians is entirely different: more relaxed and—at least in the top echelon of today's magicians—a bit more radical. I think that the immediate impact of occultism from the period that you asked about is relatively minimal. I might even go so far as to say that it made a negative impact. After all, pragmatic magic borrows some of its most significant impulses from the rebellion against exactly the type of dogmatism that Franz Bardon preached in a not-so-praiseworthy manner, which he in turn developed by borrowing from older trends on a grand scale in the 1920s.

Whew, that was another five-minute discourse on the entire history of Western magic and related world cultures; I just hope that I was at least able to answer your question. However, if you are thinking of joining an organization based on the spirit of the 1920s, then I would warn you to be careful, because things like that are not everyone's cup of tea. There is a popular saying that poorly misquotes good ole Schiller: "So look before you make a permanent commitment, you might just find something better."

I will close for now with those golden words.

Yours, Aunt Klara

WHAT ROLE DOES ASTROLOGY PLAY IN MAGIC?

DEAR AUNT KLARA, I HAVE BEEN READING YOUR COLUMN WITH GREAT INTEREST FOR QUITE SOME TIME NOW, AND I WOULD LIKE TO FINALLY ASK YOU A QUESTION MYSELF. IT IS ABOUT THE IMPORTANCE OF ASTROLOGY. MANY MAGICIANS CONSIDER THIS ART OF INTERPRETING THE STARS TO BE ONE OF THE BASIC PILLARS OF ALL WESTERN ESOTERICISM AND MAGIC. ON THE OTHER HAND, THERE ARE SOME WHO SPEAK QUITE UNFAVORABLY ABOUT IT (SUCH AS PETE CARROLL) OR IGNORE IT ALTO-GETHER (BARDON, FOR EXAMPLE). I WOULD LIKE

TO KNOW WHAT YOU THINK ABOUT THIS. MAY THE STARS ALWAYS BE ON YOUR SIDE.

HARRY Z. FROM D.

Dear Harry,

Of course, I am flattered to hear that you are a regular reader of my column. Yes, the question of astrology is indeed a bit tricky, but I am actually quite happy to see that magicians cannot seem to always agree on this point. It not only livens things up a bit, but maybe even forces people to be a bit more open-minded. After all, nothing is more detrimental to magic than the misconception that there is such a thing as an absolute truth.

Personally, I place a lot of value in astrology. I have studied this art for many years, at times even under the instruction of a teacher; I have become familiar with the heavens and hells that it has to offer us if we get involved with the aspect of forecasting important events; and I have seen what claims to accuracy it makes and how much or how little can be said of this. And even if I rarely draw up a horoscope today, I still like to entertain my friends sometimes at teatime with anecdotes from the art of interpreting the stars and astral divination, and love to talk shop with astrological experts.

But what does astrology actually have to do with magic? You can probably tell from my lengthy introduction, dear Harry Z.: I will be damned . . . um, I mean blessed . . . to bet my black un-soul to say who is right—the advocates of astrology or the opponents of this art! Of course, I could state endless arguments pro and con for combining astrology and magic, or give you some theoretical superstructure that would simply make you wiggle your dogmatic ears—but who would that be helping?

In the end, it all depends on one's personal experience and practice with the subject, and this varies from magician to magician. What I mean is that not every magician is equally skilled at astrology. One might have good knowledge of it, while another will never be able to learn it in thirty years. At least that's what I hear.

My own experience, on the other hand, says that there is no such thing as "the" art of astrology; instead, it is always what its representatives—and enemies, too!—actually make of it. My astrology teacher (with sixty years of experience!) once said that a good fifth of all birth charts cannot be interpreted in a truly reliable way. Some people are just so atypical that you would really have to grasp at straws to force a horoscope into the usual scheme of interpretation. A well-known Danish astrologer recently told me the same thing about India's astrological system. There, some Pandits hold the opinion that, although astrology is extremely precise, it almost always fails when "magic is involved"—a very informative comment, if I do say so myself!

For once I am on the same wavelength as Paul Feyerabend, when he rejects the existence of methodological rules. There is no use in explaining things away by acknowledging the existence of various techniques. One person may refer to *primary directions* while another calls them *sun arcs*. Some individuals are not at all content with the seven classical or ten modern planets; they need more, and these are even established by using a pendulum at times, as the late Mr. Witte of the Hamburg School of Astrology did. Some swear by the observation of transits, while others will not accept any interpretation that doesn't take absolutely everything into consideration—such as half-sums, fixed stars, the Galactic Center, distance-ephemerides, planetoids/asteroids, sensitive points, mirror aspects, and/or so-called hidden aspects. Even if a person is courageous enough to question astrology as a whole, he or she would first have to specify which astrological system is actually meant.

In addition, people seem to react quite differently to astrological factors. While one person may clearly feel the slightest retrograde of Mercury or a miniscule movement of the moon, another might desperately attempt to avoid an accident despite a retrograde Saturn passing over his Pluto-Mars square for the fifth time, and another may be extremely sensitive to secondary directions. Such things can also be learned, of course. It makes sense that someone who constantly deals with the planets and their influences will sooner or later actually be at their mercy.

And that brings us to a very practical matter: if you should determine that you have a certain (natural or trained) disposition for astrology, then it can be a great help to implement astrological facts into your magical practice. This will mainly consist of observing the paths of the constellations and trying to avoid unpleasant things, but you shouldn't make yourself crazy by following it too closely. A very simple comparison can be seen in the traditional practice of performing constructive magical operations during the waxing moon, while destructive operations are done during the waning moon. Accordingly, it would be symbol-logical to perform "dark" operations (as opposed to "light" operations) during lunar or solar eclipses. And astrology is certainly quite appropriate for planetary magic as well. After all, why shouldn't a person utilize a favorable Jupiter transit for charging a corresponding talisman? Or plan such an operation to be performed during this transit in the first place?

On the other hand, the whole thing has a snag, of course, and in my opinion that is the reason Bardon so deliberately ignored the subject of astrology. Namely, if you make yourself dependent on the course of the constellations through training, which some fanatics like to take to the absolute extreme at times, the apparent freedom that a magician has quickly turns into a compulsion that will cost him or her more than just a little interest fee. What use is it if I calculate that a ritual I need within the next week will not work successfully from an astrological point of view until thirty-five years from now? At any rate, magic has nothing to do with astral fatalism.

The practical solution is more likely to just take astrology for what it is—an auxiliary science that we can turn to in order to obtain information that would otherwise be much more difficult to access. After all, that is the only use magic has for anything anyway.

Now that may sound trite, but unfortunately this tidbit is disregarded way too often in everyday practice. The same thing holds true, by the way, with the limitation of the planetary hours. I remember once that a magician friend of mine was stuck in a crisis situation and desperately needed my help and that of a few other colleagues. A fast Saturn ritual was needed. "Do you really want to perform a Saturn ritual on a *Monday*?" one of them said, although I had always regarded his magical skills with a great deal of respect. This example clearly shows what a double-edged sword such Hermetic (and not only these!) tools of orientation can be. In any case, it is unquestionably better if a magician can perform his or her operations exactly when they are needed or desired instead of making them dependent on a self-imposed symbol-logical system that just gets in the way or possibly even condemns the operation to failure right from the start.

However, I also have to say that I do not particularly think highly of the mentality of some magicians who feel that they can give an opinion on astrology without ever having studied it themselves in depth. Since you have already mentioned Pete Carroll yourself, please allow me to inform you that he had quite a negative attitude about astrology in his book *Liber*

Null, but since then he has toned down his opinion a bit without directly becoming a friend of the subject. I would like to flatter myself by mentioning that I made a contribution to his change of attitude by "seeing" his wife's birthday in his own natal chart—a true act of bravura, although I willingly admit that I am not always able to perform such fabulous feats.

If a magician wants to be able to work truly independently, he or she cannot risk any type of dependency on the phases of the moon or the time of the day. That would be a contemptuous limitation of the access that all magicians aim to gain. And thus I will come to an end in the best chaos-magical way possible, by advising you only to believe in the things that are advantageous to you, and to quickly shift your paradigm as soon as you realize that it is taking its toll.

It might be a good idea also to mention that magic owes many of its most powerful symbols to astrology, in particular the planetary powers that can most certainly help us make the universe more accessible. No more, but also no less.

Solomonic salutations!
Your Aunt Klara

WHAT DO YOU THINK OF SPIRITISM AND CHANNELING?

DEAR AUNT KLARA, IT WOULD BE NICE IF YOU COULD GIVE ME YOUR OPINION ON SPIRITISM. I HAVE NOTICED THAT MOST MAGICIANS SEEM TO VIEW THIS SUBJECT WITH A BIT OF DISGUST. CROWLEY IN PARTICULAR WAS ONE OF ITS WORST FIENDS. I PERSONALLY DON'T HAVE AN OPINION ON THE SUBJECT YET, AND WOULD JUST LIKE TO CONSIDER MYSELF OPEN-MINDED HERE. HOW ABOUT YOU?

ANGELICA T. FROM W.

Dear Angelica,

Of course, my dear, everyone likes to think that they are open-minded! And your observations are correct: to most magicians, spiritism is so much of a nuisance that the psychoanalytically inclined observer could interpret that as the expression of subconscious desires. Apart from the idiotically proud dogmatists who, in their brazen ignorance, will find fault with absolutely anything occult-related, Crowley was the master of picking on spiritism, although he could not or would not avoid confronting the subject forever. After all, it is commonly known that his *Book of the Law* was dictated to him by the supernatural being Aiwass, whose existence he certainly could not deny.

On the other hand, it would be wrong to generalize and put spiritism on the same level with the spirit model of magic. After all, dealing with the spirit world is not an invention of fundamental Christian sects, even if spiritism often portrays itself in this manner. Rather, it has always been the daily bread of the shamans, and that still holds true today around the world. That is why you should take the time to examine the actual reasons behind this general rejection of spiritism. But that can be done fairly quickly and easily.

Most magicians understand "spiritism" to be the summoning of dead souls, although it is immaterial to them whether or not these souls actually exist. But magic has its own form of spiritism, too, except that there is a more elegant name for it here—*necromancy*. This is understood as the summoning of the dead for magical or divinatory purposes. But in all honesty, I really cannot see any difference between spiritism and necromancy apart from the actual procedures used. However, in order to be fair I should mention that most magicians radically reject necromancy right along with spiritism. The spectrum of arguments ranges from "One should leave the dead in peace" to the enlightened comment "Superstitious nonsense!"—and everything else in between.

But in my opinion, the main reason for the rejection of spiritism since the turn of the twentieth century seems to be Christianity itself. Even back during the Renaissance, it was the good practice of every magician to summon the spirits of the dead into his or her temple, and in doing so, it was popular practice to call upon well-known personalities. That has hardly changed throughout the years in all cultures throughout the world—even among the shamans.

Spiritism is surely as old as humanity itself, but the form that we know it as today is a product of the nineteenth century, more specifically of Protestant piety. After taking root in the United States, like many other disastrous things, it managed to find a new home—strangely enough, in staid, sober-minded England. There it was integrated into everyday religious life by Christian groups that were formally considered unorthodox, but in reality were quite conformist. Many magicians today are completely unaware that Arthur Conan Doyle, the inventor of Sherlock Holmes and an honest British gentleman born and bred (though being born a Catholic in Anglican England made him a permanent social outsider and a potential underdog), was actually one of the most significant figures of spiritism around the time of the First World War—something that Aleister Crowley naturally held against him.

This specific form of spiritism that prefers to call itself "spiritualism" is, in my opinion, nothing more than a religiously cloaked romanticism of the afterlife. Even today, one can take part in public sessions of the Spiritualist Association of Great Britain that are held regularly at London's Belgrave Square. The former president of this group—namely, Tom Johanson—was ironically a student of Austin Osman Spare (at least during the 1980s, according to my knowledge). So the apple really does not fall far from the tree!

In addition, spiritism was unfortunately haunted by a plague of charlatanism around the turn of the twentieth century. In an attempt to get to the bottom of the phenomenon of spirit materialization, scientists back then, who were even more naïve than they are today, fell by the bundles into the traps of tricksters—one of the more famous swindlers, according to known evidence, being the sly Madame Blavatsky. And as one scam after another was exposed, there was not an intelligent soul left who wanted to be associated with this movement. After all, the very limited number of magicians who actually had a brain in their head almost always considered it to be way too folksy and intellectually inferior.

This opinion is certainly vindicated when a person hears one of the many trivialities that are apparently still typical to spiritism today. Like the deceased grandfather who happily reports from the afterlife that he can even get his favorite brand of cigars "over there"—and that is an unequivocally true case that has been documented!

Today it is referred to by the more American but no less finer name of "channeling," and in such channeling circles, there are often reports of Aleister Crowley and other such villains posthumously regretting their derogatory statements on the subject in a sort of "afterlife conversion."

It may be that a sole magician here or there gets an interesting tip for his or her own magical practice, for all I care by tapping into the informational field of a prominent ancestor of our art. But first of all, that would certainly be a diminishing minority, and secondly, in my opinion, neither spiritism nor necromancy has ever really contributed anything significant to magic. A cynic once said, "How do we know that the people in the afterlife are not just as dumb as when they were alive?" After all, death is no cure for stupidity.

With ghastly greetings,
Your Aunt Klara

Eliphas Lévi—an "enlightened master" of magic?

Dear Aunt Klara, I would be much obliged if you could find a place in your column to honor the contribution of Eliphas Lévi. Nowadays there is not too much talk about this enlightened master of magic.

JOHANNES M. FROM B.

Dear Johannes,

Let me take a good swing at the traditionalists for a change. First, let's make one thing clear: today more people *talk* about Eliphas Lévi than actually read his works. That is no wonder, considering that what he actually had to say about magical practice is quite meager. It appears that throughout his lifetime he only ever performed one single ritual at most—or at least he never mentions more than one (which failed by the way): namely, his conjuration of Apollonius of Tyana, a necromantic job that he performed for someone else during which he quickly got cold feet. Honestly, I always find it quite tiring to browse through his books. Nonetheless, he sweetens the dullness a bit by setting many tracks that are certainly not all dead ends, which is personally quite interesting to me with my excellent historical background (hear, hear!).

I would not view him as "enlightened," but rather as a "lighter," and I do not mean that condescendingly. Try to imagine the time in which he lived: magic was dormant, rationalism flexed its freshly oiled muscles all over the place, and many an optimist thought that organized religions were nearing their end. The newest fad was Charles Darwin, who reduced man to his basic biological measurements, which irritated theology immensely since it viewed its highly praised human being as both a servant and the center of all salvation. And if one could truly talk about something such as practical magic, this was at best limited to the relatively haphazard operations of folk magicians and their clients.

As everyone knows, Lévi himself was quite a problematic figure. By the way, he was not a Catholic priest in the true sense of the word—as many people claim even today, regardless of the fact that he gave *himself* the title of "abbé" (abbot). Although he was ordained into lower offices, for various reasons he never actually obtained priesthood. Like his contemporary (and even ancestor in a sense) Edgar Allan Poe, he was the prototype of "bourgeois bohemia." Despite having an adversity to every type of regular activity, he nonetheless excelled in what we know today as PR work.

Let us not forget the fact that, in those days, it was improper for a gentleman or man of status (which Lévi was not really, at least according to his social background) to work for his own living. But that does not mean that Lévi was not diligent and industrious. I would like to refrain from gossiping on about his biography, though, and focus on the role that he played in magic and still does to some extent today.

Lévi was responsible for two great achievements. First, he made magic in general socially acceptable again, and second, he was one of the first to make a connection between the tarot and the kabbalistic Tree of Life. If there were any forerunners for that, I am not aware of them. Of course, the speculative Kabbalah corresponded completely to the intellectual and yet romanticized spiritual climate at the time, in general but also specifically in France. In his book *Monde primitif*, published just fifty years beforehand, Antoine Court de Gébelin claimed that the tarot was the secret book of knowledge of the ancient Egyptians (the legendary *Book of Thot*). And then Lévi again picked up the thread of the Hebrew aspect (which lies closer to Christianity anyway), along with the corresponding consequences that we still have to deal with today, either to our pleasure or dissatisfaction, depending on one's personal opinion.

Beyond that, Lévi was one of the first to write a summary of the history of magic that was both comprehensive as well as appropriately coherent, albeit with a lack of accuracy in detail. His influence on occultists of the time can hardly be downplayed. He was good friends with Bulwer-Lytton, the author of such earth-shattering works as *Zanoni* and *Vril* and also one of the leading figures in Britain's Rosicrucianism. His student was Papus (a.k.a. Gérard Encausse), who in turn was the occult advisor for Czar Nicholas II's court. Aleister Crowley declared himself to be a reincarnation of Lévi. Mathers and A. E. White were also among his admirers, as were William Butler Yeats and Rudolf Steiner. He influenced Péladan as well as Przybyszewski and Guaita. Ah, the list goes on and on!

Now, there are two possible explanations for the strong influence that Eliphas Lévi undeniably had on others. The first is inherent in magic and says that he was supposedly a high initiate; this is surely a convenient answer since no one is able to prove the contrary. Personally, I like the taste of the second explanation much better. It says that Lévi was mainly an ingenious magician-journalist, a synoptic visionary who understood how to tap the pulse of the times with immense precision and to close the gap in the market with the perfect subject at just the right moment.

This may sound derogatory, but it is not intended to be. On the contrary, I take my hat off to anyone who manages to open up so many perspectives in magic as Lévi did. Even if he cannot be counted among the great practical experts of our art, given a lack of evidence to the contrary and based on the reading material in his often quite muddled and inconsistent *Introduction to Magic*, I nonetheless admire his ability to give the magic of his era an entirely new, mysterious, and yet easily accessible aura, allowing it to truly become *alive* in the imagination of his contemporaries. This is without a doubt an unparalleled pioneering venture.

He has been accused of romanticizing magic, and I have to agree with this opinion. On the other hand, who didn't romanticize things back then? It was a characteristic of the blossoming neo-Romanticism period that reached its climax during the late Symbolism movement at the turn of the last century. His entire work is without a doubt more original and advanced than the highly overestimated Francis Barrett, whose book *The Magus* (published in London in 1801) is nothing more than a brewed-up Agrippa, written by a gentlemanly dilettante who knew how to make a few quick guineas.

I already said that Lévi's more or less "legendary" status is surely much larger than the actual number of his readers. If his writing seems a bit intricate and complicated today, especially to younger magicians, then it is most certainly due in part to the clumsy translations of his works that are available to us (by the way, A. E. Waite's English translations are just as awkward as the German translations), as well as to the fact that he conveys the feeling to his readers that they *might* be high initiates if only they could learn to read between the lines and understand the signs.

There are magicians who appreciate Lévi for his theory of "astral light," a concept that comes fairly close to Bulwer's *vril* or Reichenbach's *od*, and which possibly even influenced these.

Indeed, this man probably deserves a lot more to be said about him, but I would rather wrap this up now before it turns into a doctoral thesis. Please do not be angry with me if everything I've said about your pillar saint was not all that good. After all, as a fierce, coffee-addicted old biddy, that's just my style.

Not one bit remorseful,
Your Aunt Klara

DID THE O.T.O. "INVENT" SEX MAGIC?

My dearest Aunt Klara, Everyone knows that it is difficult to imagine the history of modern magic without mentioning the O.T.O. This brotherhood is often described as one of the "inventors" of sex magic, and I have heard rumors that it has integrated not only Eastern but also American (!) influences into its system. Can you tell me more about that? I would be pleased for any detailed information that you can divulge.

Franz L. from N.

Dear Franz,

You are certainly grasping a hot iron there, and even if you would like a detailed answer from me—which flatters me, of course—I can only tell you what I have heard from hearsay myself, albeit from fairly reliable sources. You are correct in the fact that most literature on the subject generally assumes that the O.T.O. bases its sex magic entirely on the inspiration Karl Kellner got on his journeys to the Middle East and Central Asia.

At this point, I do not want to get into the fairly controversial issue of when the order was actually founded; after all, it has had quite a turbulent past and was not spared from the corresponding myths and legends surrounding it either. Theodor Reuss, a close confidant of Kellner's, and theosophist Franz Hartmann, who was employed as a doctor in Kellner's sanatorium, surely contributed much more to the O.T.O. than their mentor. But of course it is no secret that the order surely would never have become what it is (or means) today without Aleister Crowley having taken over.

Karl Kellner was a stinking-rich inventor and manufacturer who held over a hundred patents—a truly rare personality among the usual flock of occultist have-nots! Among other things, he advanced the procedure of making paper from wood as well as the corresponding electrolytic whitening process. Together with British industrialist Edward Partington, he founded the Kellner-Partington Paper Pulp Company, with its headquarters in Manchester and branch offices in both Norway and the Austrian city of Hallein. In Hallein, located in the Salzkammergut region, the company established its main production site—a factory that is still partially preserved today. Kellner was also buried in this ancient Celtic stronghold, and it is one of the ironies of the magical world that he lies in a Catholic grave decorated with a concealed symbol of Rosicrucianism. It is said that he received his training in yoga from a guru in Lahore, where he supposedly also acquired his knowledge of Tantrism.

Right next to the factory in Hallein, an inhalatorium was built that produced the cellulose waste product lignosulfite, which was then used to treat tuberculosis patients. There is hardly a more practical form of recycling! Franz Hartmann, who was having financial difficulties following the decline of theosophy, was hired by Kellner to work there as a doctor. Thus, little by little, such illustrious personalities as Lou Andreas-Salomé,

Gustav Meyrink, and Theodor Reuss, as already mentioned, began to meet and assemble. Kellner owned a villa in Vienna with an "alchemistic observatory" (laboratory?) and a tantric devotion room. A few photographs have survived from this time, since Kellner was also a pioneer in the field of color photography.

Sex magic is naturally not a modern-day invention. Just look at the temple prostitution of Babylonia and India, the pre-Aryan Tantrism of the Dravidians, the countless fertility rites in all world cultures, the ophitish sperm gnosis, the Ortlibians and the Brethren of the Free Spirit of medieval times, certain Jewish and Islamic (in particular Sufi) practices, and maybe even the alleged (and speculative) sexual rites of the Knights Templar—sex magic flourished just about everywhere. The O.T.O., however, is an exception, in that it is an obliged brotherhood with structures and symbols similar to that of Freemasonry.

It might also be interesting to note that Kellner thought himself to be the reincarnation of a Babylonian fire priest. An "occult club" then came into being in Vienna, which was the forerunner of the O.T.O. and only accessible to high-ranking Masons from the Rite of Memphis-Misraim. They also maintained contact with the Vienna branch of the Brotherhood of

Luxor, which practiced sex magic as well. That makes an interesting link to Aleister Crowley, who was still a member of the Golden Dawn at the time. Within this British order, another inner circle had formed around Crowley's good friend Frank Harris, who also maintained contact with the Brotherhood of Luxor. This brotherhood is an order founded by Paschal Beverly Randolph, a mixed-race American from New York who was also the author of *Magia sexualis*, a book on the subject of sex magic that was quite revolutionary for its time, yet is, in my opinion, also highly overrated. Viennese artist and satanologist Josef Dvorak had read Czech translations of Randolph's work, as he once personally told me. These volumes, which were printed in Prague, were repeatedly put on the index of disapproved books by the police in the region around the Austrian border. Nonetheless, at least one state-censored edition was published in Vienna as well.

Francis King pointed out the highly underrated role that Edward Sellon played in Victorian England through the propagation of Tantrism and Arabic-influenced sex magic. Another significant orientalist was Sir Richard Francis Burton, who was greatly admired by Crowley. He was an expert in the field of erotic literature of the East as well as a talented translator, among other things. Unfortunately, very little practical material remains of Burton's works because his widow destroyed all of his "risqué" manuscripts after his death, an act that made Crowley absolutely furious.

The sex-magic and mystical currents in America have apparently been criminally neglected as well. In their biography of Reuss, Helmut Möller and Ellic Howe refer to the lesser known Reverend Kenneth Sylvan Launfal Guthrie (such names happen to be allowed in the land of unlimited opportunities). This man seems to have rediscovered for himself the Indian and Chinese practices of tantra and inner alchemy without any knowledge of their Eastern origins. His book *Regeneration: The Gate of Heaven* was published in 1897. He also founded the "Brotherhood of the Eternal Covenant," which advertised to help seekers "find the right path to sexualistic vitalism," as Möller and Howe put it. Of course, there were other libertine currents that prevailed in the United States, at least for a while, despite—or maybe because of— the general puritan mood of society at the time, the most significant of these being the quasi-anarchistic

Oneida Community, as well as numerous other religiously disguised splinter groups.

Now Freemasonry, of course, was often accused by its opponents of implementing unspeakable sexual practices—ancient persecution tactics that have prevailed well before the witch-hunts and the wiping out of the Order of the Knights Templar. Still, even today there is no absolute certainty (although it is quite likely) that the libertinistic gnosis really did exist during the age of early Christianity. The accounts of gnostic orgies and other sexual excesses in a ritualistic context stem for the most part from the Christian enemies of the gnostics.

But it is not my intention to go into that here. I think it is much more important to note that the O.T.O. was a quasi-Masonic association that had close ties to the Rite of Memphis-Misraim, which Crowley regarded quite highly. Also, the O.T.O. adopted sex magic in a ritually formalized way that led to the development of its own unique style; and of course it was the O.T.O. that publicly propagated this discipline as well. So in Crowley's autobiography, when he pretends he was entirely inexperienced in the field of sex magic until he had met Reuss and through him first learned of the great significance of sexuality in magic, then that is either a downright lie or at least a bit twisted in truth. As has been pointed out a few times before, it's also a bit strange that he did not mention Arthur Avalon in any of his books. After all, Avalon—whose real name was Sir John Woodroffe—was a justice of the peace in India in his day as well as a highly respected researcher of Tantrism. It seems next to impossible that Crowley was not aware of Woodroffe's works (e.g., on kundalini yoga, chakra letter magic, and modern Bengali Tantrism) that were published around the turn of the twentieth century. After all, if there ever were a truly sharp-eyed observer on the scene who also had the necessary leisure time to pursue every aspect of his discipline, then it was surely Aleister Crowley. On the other hand, it is difficult to understand why he would have concealed such an influence, or at least the acknowledgment thereof. Because Crowley was not at all the type to conceal his sources.

In any case, dear Franz, you are entirely correct in pursuing this matter. We have seen that there is still a lot of roadwork to be done here. So if you would like to combine instinct with scholarship (and a leaden butt for studying the vast amount of literature!), then those of us historically interested in the magic scene would certainly be quite grateful. In any case, I can safely say already that the early O.T.O. must have had strong American influences, in particular in the field of sex magic. One thing that strikes me as strange, though, is the fact that Crowley never mentions Randolph (who was an American) at all, at least to my knowledge.

I am truly sorry if I have made the whole matter more complicated for you, but you really cannot hold me responsible for the lack of available resources. Maybe it is just time for me to put in a few semesters of research again, which I certainly plan to do just as soon as my money demons finally procure enough mammon for me so that I can live entirely off the interest.

In hopeful expectation,
Your Aunt Klara

WHAT PURPOSE DOES THE RITUAL BURNING OF INCENSE FULFILL?

DEAR AUNT KLARA! I WOULD LIKE TO KNOW MORE ABOUT THE EXACT FUNCTION OF BURNING INCENSE DURING RITUALS. WOULD YOU BE ABLE TO HELP ME?

ELFRIEDE P. FROM G.

Dear Elfriede,

Your question is a bit vague, but let me see what I can do. Actually the answer is quite simple: incense puts the magician into a certain frame of mind that is commonly known as gnosis, or magical trance. When using certain mixtures (such as planetary incense and the like), the intention is to stimulate the related psycho-magical associations, thus activating the corresponding powers. Maybe you already know that the sense of smell has a direct connection to the oldest part of the brain—namely, the brain stem, or "lizard" brain. This is why scents and smells can lead to fairly predictable reactions when skillfully applied by knowledgeable persons. That is how the perfume industry makes a living, and not a bad one at that!

The smoke can also be used for cleansing and purification, such as is done during Catholic rites and in Asian temples. However, I cannot tell you what the "right" substance is to use for which purpose, since this field in particular places no value in standardizing hermetic tradition. In nine out of ten cases, experts will categorize one and the same substance into principally different groups or powers. That is why it is important here to heed the good ole basic principle of pragmatic magic: the initiate is better off by experimenting and creating his or her own experiences instead of automatically assuming someone else's ideas.

Apart from cleansing and generating a state of trance (or "creating the right mood"), the smoke of incense can also be used for shamanic journeys. For example, it is known that Siberian shamans like to use a cloud of smoke for their nonphysical travels; this cloud is used to carry them to the desired location in the spirit world.

And finally, let me mention one more function of incense. In the conjuring of demons, it is known that the manifestation of these scaly creatures requires at least the consistency of thick vapors. Here, incense (sometimes called the "sweat of the gods" in older texts) serves as both an offering and as a material basis for the sensory expression in concrete terms. Even in ancient books of spells, one can find indications of how to project images of demons from the altar into a column of smoke by using a system of mirrors that resembles a projector. That was not intended to be a trick of deception, though. After all, who would be able to deceive someone this way in the long term? Instead, it served to aid visualization because of the way the smoke wavers and can bring an image to life when cleverly projected onto it.

Many magicians use incense as a signal for the start of a trance (or the shift to a different one) and design their rituals accordingly. In this way, planetary incense would be used immediately before the particular planetary powers are invoked, while before and after that a general, cleansing mixture could be used.

But in the end, incense mixtures are merely tools of magic—just like daggers, swords, chalices, pentacles, wands, and even the temple itself, and a magician should be careful not to become too dependent on these.

With fragrant greetings,
Your Aunt Klara

ASTRAL TRAVEL—
HOW DOES IT WORK?

DEAR AUNT KLARA, FOR QUITE SOME TIME NOW
I HAVE BEEN TRYING TO SEPARATE MY ASTRAL
BODY BY USING THE FOLLOWING METHOD: I LIE
FLAT ON MY BACK, BREATH DEEPLY AND SLOWLY,
AND ENTER A STATE OF DEEP RELAXATION, AS I
LEARNED TO DO THROUGH AUTOGENIC TRAINING.
THEN I TRY TO SEPARATE MY ASTRAL BODY FROM
MY PHYSICAL BODY UNTIL IT FLOATS ROUGHLY A
FOOT AND A HALF ABOVE ME. BUT I STILL HAVE
NOT HAD ANY LUCK, ALTHOUGH I HAVE BEEN
PRACTICING SEVERAL TIMES A DAY FOR MONTHS.
I READ THAT ONE SHOULD SHIFT HIS OR HER
AWARENESS TO THE ASTRAL BODY TO BE ABLE TO

FUNCTION IN IT. BUT HOW EXACTLY CAN THAT WORK IF I AM NOT EVEN SURE WHETHER I AM OUT OF MY BODY OR NOT? WHAT SHOULD I DO? CAN YOU HELP?

SIGURD V. FROM B.

Dear Sigurd,

Lots of magicians struggle with the same problem, beginners in particular. That may not offer much consolation, but maybe I have some tips that will help. The technique you described for astral travel is surely the most common. For some people it works in just a short time, but not for everyone. That may be due to insufficient imagination training, but of course that does not help the affected person very much.

Maybe you could try the following exercise instead: Determine a location that you want to visit astrally. Instead of lying down, sit in a comfortable position. (As with any type of astral work, it is important here that you make sure that you will not be disturbed. Because if a dear family member bursts into the room or the dachshund insists on being let outside, this can have a subtle yet long-lasting negative effect on your practice.) Now expand your body roughly half an inch with each breath. This is done only in the imagination, is fairly easy to do, and often produces fast results.

When you have expanded to roughly twice your normal size, continue the process with even greater dimensions. Inches become feet, and feet become miles, and so on. Don't worry too much about the actual act of leaving your body, since that's not what it is really about. After all, a person usually wants to travel astrally in order to perform a sort of remote divination—e.g., to determine what a good friend is currently doing for the purpose of remote healing. Therefore, remember that it is not necessarily all about the astral body. Personally, I tend to speculate that this ominous astral body is nothing more than a myth at best, one that makes it easier for us to tap into specific information from often faraway, remote sources.

One variation of this technique consists of proceeding little by little. For example, the first few times you would only move your astral arms out of your physical body, a bit later your whole upper body and head, and so on. But if you really only want to find out how your friend in the Canary Islands is doing, then always keep in mind that obtaining this remote information is your actual goal, regardless of how you get there, and not necessarily the act of buzzing around in an astral body. That should at least prevent any type of tension or grim determination.

Experienced magicians often do without astral travel altogether, since it is comparatively complicated whereas the desired information can often be obtained much faster and easier. However, this does not mean that a person should renounce astral travel altogether. On the contrary, this practice often leads to a greater exposure to what we like to call "intuition," for lack of a better word and without truly understanding its origin.

This concept of having various human bodies, which was borrowed from theosophy, is surely a useful tool that everyone can relate to fairly well. But that's still no reason to cling to it for eternity. Therefore, formulate your goals specifically. Determine for yourself what it is that you actually want to achieve, and if your practice gets dull, then just try something different for a while, as described here.

Hovering and floating,
Your Aunt Klara

WHAT ROLE DOES SHAMANISM PLAY IN CONTEMPORARY MAGIC?

DEAR AUNT KLARA! I HAVE BEEN STUDYING MODERN PRACTICAL MAGIC FOR QUITE SOME TIME NOW AND NATURALLY I KEEP COMING ACROSS THE SUBJECT OF SHAMANISM. BUT WHAT DO I MEAN BY "NATURALLY"? I'M NOT NECESSARILY CHAUVINISTIC OR FIXATED ON OUR OWN WESTERN CULTURE, BUT SOMETIMES I ASK MYSELF WHETHER THE MODERN EUROPEAN MAGICIAN REALLY HAS TO FOLLOW EVERY AMERICAN TREND. WHEN I SEE THE KINDS OF PEOPLE IN GERMANY WHO CALL THEMSELVES "SHAMANS"; WHEN I TALK TO

PEOPLE WHO INSIST THAT THEY HAVE TO BECOME
CELTIC INDIAN WITCHES IN ORDER TO RESTORE
ECOLOGICAL BALANCE TO THE RAINBOW PLANET
WITH TIBETAN ATLANTIS RUNES . . . WELL, AD-
MITTEDLY, THESE ARE EXTREME FANATICAL MOVE-
MENTS AND NOT NECESSARILY RELIGIOUS ONES,
BUT THEY DO CONVEY A GREAT DEAL OF MAGICAL
CONCEPTS, EVEN IF THEY AVOID CALLING IT THAT
DIRECTLY. BUT IS THERE ANY TRUTH TO ALL THE
FUSS? WHEN I LOOK AT THE ETHNOLOGIC LITERA-
TURE AVAILABLE, IT SEEMS THAT THE SHAMANS
OF SO-CALLED PRIMITIVE CULTURES OR INDIG-
ENOUS TRIBES WERE PREDOMINANTLY NARROW-
MINDED DOGMATISTS. OH, SORRY, I REALLY
WASN'T PLANNING TO WRITE AN ESSAY HERE; I
JUST WANTED TO ASK HOW YOU VIEW THE SIG-
NIFICANCE OF SHAMANISM IN MODERN MAGIC.

WOLFGANG W. FROM W.

Dear Wolfgang,

You've poked a bit of fun at the matter, which I think
is quite appropriate. The "rainbow" culture of "New
Age" apostles is indeed unintentionally comical at
times. But please try to avoid idealizing the past to get
one over on the present, because otherwise you will
eventually lose all access to the future! I am not implying that this has already happened, and I can certainly

understand that you might prefer less of a "melting pot" atmosphere in the magical culture of Western Europe. But please do not forget that occultism, and magic in particular, has always been a reservoir for taking on the most diverse cultural movements. This is called *syncretism*. Syncretism means that, out of all the possible trends and movements out there, a person picks and chooses only that which he or she can actually use, or thinks can be used.

Even back in ancient times, one could find corrupted forms of Egyptian, Sumerian, and pre-Socratic elements of magic, all colorfully mixed together with Hebrew formulas and folk magic—enough to make any culturally squeaky-clean person have some serious fun trying to tidy up the Augean stables. When observed with the proper distance, the strict boundaries disappear and we see a single unity that is and was actually quite heterogeneous.

Today we can already observe new currents while they are in the making. Now, however, we have a different problem—namely, that it is increasingly difficult for us to detach ourselves from the system of order that we have grown so fond of, although such detachment is indeed necessary for the old to be able to merge with the new.

But what does shamanism actually have to offer modern magic? Well, quite a bit, such as its highly advanced trance technology that makes our so-called "consciousness explorers" look like incompetent children, as well as a purely advantage-oriented pragmatism of the most radical type from which many of us could learn a few things—especially those of us who tend to flee into the world of speculation a bit too quickly and prematurely. Indigenous tribes are not just romantic dreamers who spend the whole day enraptured by sniffing at sweet little flowers, but instead they are practitioners of the first degree. At the place where dogma starts sneaking its way into the picture, decadence is already well underway, but that seems to be an indispensable side effect of any type of "civilization." When groups of people reach a certain critical mass, it is essential to have some form of management in addition to a chief. The "shamanic" aspect of so-called indigenous tribes is mainly the fact that the sorcerer holds a relatively high position within the chain of command. Later, in papal states, this chief is replaced by a high priest.

Thus it would be quite naïve to define something like "love of nature" as a characteristic of shamanism. When indigenous people talk about the "good Mother

Earth," we can be certain that they have already been corrupted by Rousseauian ideals. These are so-called "apple Indians"—red on the outside, white on the inside. The simple preservation of an ecological balance in the interest of one's own survival is an entirely different thing. There is nothing "lovely" about that, yet it provides all the more access.

But we should get back to talking about shamanism now and its significance to magic. I will start with the magical-trance techniques already mentioned above that had been long forgotten in the Western tradition. Right up through the 1970s, the magical literature of our civilization contains the formula "magic = will + imagination," which can be used to easily explain such baby-soft magical techniques as "positive thinking." But through our contact with shamanism (or neo-shamanism, to be more specific), we now have to extend this formula by the factor of "trance" or "altered state of consciousness." Our interest in the drug practices of the indigenous tribes certainly contributed to this.

We have also long forgotten about the natural and even routine way that magic is practiced in shamanic cultures. The key phrase *integration of magic into everyday life* should be enough to illustrate what I mean by this. In places where shamanism is still "genuine," it is always pragmatically oriented. No tribal sorcerer would have second thoughts about a sentence such as *The main thing is that it works*, as opposed to many hermetic/kabbalistic magicians who are searching endlessly for an absoluteness that is never more closely defined. From this point of view, working with shamanism has certainly shaken up dogmatic positions, razed castles to the ground, and torn down protective walls that would have otherwise imprisoned us in a system of efficiency avoidance.

By the way, society's modern conflict about the distribution of raw materials is definitely not a foreign concept to shamanism. In earlier days, it was about the securing of hunting grounds, pastures, arable land, and the like. In this sense, true shamanism puts a lot more emphasis on power than documented Western magic does, with the exception of the evocation of demons. Presumably, all magic can be derived from primeval hunting sorcery, as it was mainly about ensuring one's own survival, taking over territory, and expanding one's range of access. It goes without saying that weather magic obviously played an important role in the earliest of times, just as everything else did that we now describe with the trendy term *survival*.

The cultural denseness that we can observe among so-called shamans despite all of the mentioned pragmatism is mainly due to the fact that the shaman has not yet managed to accomplish the Western process that we call "division of labor." The shaman is not only a sorcerer, but also a historian, theologian, pastor, doctor, and quite often the appointed judge in the community. And so it happens that the shaman, as a true crossover artist, first has to develop appropriate rules and models of explanation for the magically knowledgeable people he or she is responsible for. But it is a well-known fact that any true practitioners—whether they belong to indigenous tribes or civilized nations—frequently need to abandon all dogmas and rules in cases of doubt if they want efficiency. That probably applies to all areas of human action, though it is much more apparent in the fields of magic, religion, warfare, and political realism.

In summary, I would like to say that shamanism has surely shaken us out of our reverie regardless of the many "seminar" side effects that may not really seem genuine. Plus, it has also opened our eyes to the significance of folk magic, which many magicians have long denounced in their own cultural struggle, as can be seen repeatedly in the efforts put into distancing themselves from the "superstitions of the dumb guys." I certainly have no intention of transfiguring anything here. After all, when I hear such things I automatically think of the nice saying by Karl Kraus: "Vox populi, vox blockhead," but what actually takes place in the lower levels of society's structure is at times quite a refreshing cultural disgrace. It is more ideological and less political—anarchy in its pure form. So regardless of whatever those learned gentlemen in their kabbalistic/hermetic libraries come up with and proclaim to be the absolute truth, a shepherd in the remote mountains will still cuddle a fetish, the village witch will still whisper spells over the warts of clients, and people will still bury mandrake at the crossroads at midnight, or hang horseshoes over doorways to protect lightning from striking, and so on.

And finally, there is one more connection between primeval shamanism and modern magic that should not be underestimated. I am talking about the work with atavisms as popularized in the West by Austin Osman Spare. It is a well-known fact that Spare himself admitted to being initiated into magic as a child by an old witch named Peterson. And anyone who examines Spare's idiosyncratic system a bit more closely would certainly feel inclined to believe him.

Work with animals and animal powers, with animal trance and animal relics, has clearly always been typical of shamanism. Such concepts could only rarely be found in advanced civilizations, such as in ancient Egypt. The shaman makes practical use of the animal while the theologian wants to *conquer* it. Now, most of us know from our own experience that working with "atavistic nostalgia," or "atavistic revival" as Spare once demonstrated, is not only extremely effective, but can also be a whole lot of fun. That is probably the reason why the old dogmatists of the angular tradition of magic like to turn up their nose at such things.

The beginnings of the intense involvement with Spare's atavistic magic and with shamanism lie barely a decade apart, which in magical terms is hardly nothing at all. Both sprouted from the fertile ground that was fairly well cultivated by the Wicca movement, starting in the 1950s. The interest that some people have in the Native Americans can also be understood as a part of this spiritual current. Without these predecessors to pave the way, modern-day chaos magic would have been unthinkable—a fact that just may surprise a few of you!

To my knowledge, chaos magic in its organized form—namely, the IOT or "Pact"—developed a group structure not unlike that of the Wicca tradition. This includes the autonomy of an individual temple. Possibly more significant, though, is that chaos magic is just as group-specific and anarchic as the Wicca movement. Of course, that should not disguise the fact that chaos magic owes quite a bit to more modern movements as well, such as quantum physics, philosophical structuralism/relativism, the "Discordian movement," hippie and rock culture, and the science-fiction scene.

So have I utterly confused you now? After first taking up the cudgels for syncretism, which often undertakes an attempt to observe everything from a "holistic" point of view, I have now reduced the whole thing to its component parts. By doing so, I only wanted to make it clear that when syncretism propagates such a simplistic, uniform view of things, then (in my opinion) it can only lead to undesired dead ends at best. But if its attack on the various, heterogeneous systems is a conscious one, this is what actually gives it a practical driving force.

But whoever wants to tritely interpret this as the "unity of all things" is confusing something here.

Surely, quantum physics makes it increasingly clear that everything is somehow related. But in no way does that mean that everything is the same! At the risk of possibly provoking wrong associations here, I would nonetheless like to mention Crowley's "Every man and woman is a star" in this context—not in the sense of a gigantic, cosmic clockwork that compels us to fatalistic, deterministic assimilation, but rather as an individual in the collective that goes well beyond any type of socially required isolation to ever-shrinking associations (small families, clubs and committees, and so forth).

At least shamanism can help shift the focus of all magical action back to functionality again, and even to help us recognize our actual link to all bio-organisms on this planet without transfiguring them.

But before I lose myself in the seamy side of philosophy and the critique of contemporary civilization, I had better stop here. After all, it is almost time for coffee, and I have more important ritual chickens to pluck!

Shaking my rattle like crazy,
Your Aunt Klara

DO THE HARRY POTTER NOVELS CONTAIN MAGICAL INSIDE KNOWLEDGE?

DEAR AUNT KLARA, MY KIDS ARE BIG HARRY POTTER FANS, AND I EVEN READ EACH NEW BOOK AS SOON AS IT WAS PUBLISHED. I ADMIRE J. K. ROWLING'S USE OF LANGUAGE AND HOW SHE MAKES THE CHARACTERS SEEM SO REAL. BUT SOMETIMES I CANNOT HELP THINKING THAT HER WORLD OF MAGIC IS NOT AS FAR-FETCHED AS IT MIGHT SEEM AT FIRST GLANCE. DO YOU THINK THAT THE AUTHOR HAS "REAL" CONNECTIONS TO THE BRITISH MAGIC SCENE? OR DID SHE JUST

**GET THIS INFORMATION BY READING UP ON IT:
A SOMEWHAT DOPEY WIZARD PRIEST WEARING
A PINSTRIPED CAPE; EVIL PURE-BLOODED SOR-
CERERS FROM AN ANCIENT LINEAGE OF WITCHES
THAT DISLIKE "MUDBLOODS"; THE ORDER OF THE
PHOENIX; THE WISE, ALMOST HOLY DUMBLEDORE
(OK, HE COULD HAVE COME STRAIGHT OUT OF A
FAIRY TALE); AND THE EVER-SO-EVIL AND DIS-
LOYAL LORD VOLDEMORT WHO WAS ONCE A VERY
PROMISING YOUNG MAN . . . THINGS LIKE THAT
CANNOT JUST SIMPLY BE MADE UP. OR CAN THEY?
WHAT DO YOU THINK?**

JULIANE M. FROM B.

My dear Juliane,

You have placed your curious little witch's finger right on the pulse of the times! I have been asking myself for years why no one from the so-called "magic scene" (or whatever is left of it right now) has ever asked me about Harry Potter and his creator. On the other hand, maybe I already know the answer—just wait and see!

You know, such thoughts are not entirely new: whenever an author writes about magical content in such a captivating and convincing way (and I am talking about storytelling novels here, not nonfiction), people wonder whether said author might have some kind of practical experience or possibly even be "initiated" into some high circle.

This suspicion is not all that outlandish; after all, a great number of occultists and magicians were indeed authors of literature as well, writing about their experiences in the form of a novel—sometimes blunt and direct, other times in a complicated and indirect manner. Even the *Chymical Wedding of Christian Rosencreutz*, which is still today a core piece of literature within the Rosicrucian movement, was written in storytelling prose—and is often viewed by some naïve individuals as a true, factual account. The list of such works and their authors is long, and I only want to pick out a few specific ones here to support my statements, not to make a doctoral thesis out of the subject.

We have British Rosicrucian and magician Bulwer-Lytton and his novel *Zanoni*, or the *Faust* drama by Freemason Goethe, the novel *Dhoula Bel* from American sex magician Paschal Beverly Randolph, the theatrical play *Axël* by Villiers de L'Isle-Adam, or the various works by Gustav Meyrink, ranging from *The Golem* to *The Green Face* to *The Angel of the West Window*—these are all books of occult and often magical content (which is not always the same) that were written by more or less expert authorities of the material. We also need to mention Aleister Crowley's *Moonchild*, *The Sea Priestess* by Dion Fortune, and Gerald Brosseau Gardner, of course, with his *High Magic's Aid*—a book that led to the birth of the whole new Pagan/Wicca movement. Finally, maybe I should mention the sex magic novel *Exorial*, written by the founder of the Fraternitas Saturni, Gregor A. Gregorius, who claimed that the original manuscript for this book was "misappropriated" by no one less than the head of the Swiss O.T.O., Joseph Metzger. Some magicians may want to mention *Initiation* by Elisabeth Haich, as well as *The Red Lion* by Maria Szepes. But then that should be enough.

As you see, there are a number of examples for magical "insiders" who have tried their hand at literature. However, the number of non-occultists who have dealt with magical themes in their literature is much greater. Here, too, I only want to mention a few choice examples in order to illustrate what I will be explaining a bit further on. And since we are talking about examples here, maybe you should follow mine and get yourself a nice cup of hot coffee, as black as the darkest Satanic lodge, before we continue . . .

In his novel *Alraune*, Hanns Heinz Ewers clearly falls back on magical themes, but I am not aware of him ever being an active occultist or having anything whatsoever to do with magic.

Tolkien was an academic researcher of myths and legends, but certainly not an occultist. Nonetheless, his *Lord of the Rings* can certainly be considered magical literature. Thomas Mann may have occupied himself with spiritism for a while, though merely in a passive sense, but that is about all. Again and again, people claim that his book *The Magic Mountain* is a "hermetic story"—which may even be indirectly true. (By that I am implying that you should not necessarily trust the authors themselves in this sense; often they are only convincing themselves that they are dealing with magical, occult content when in reality the magical aspect is limited to a handful of amazing effects and characters loosely borrowed from the magical world. Such as Somerset Maugham in his book *The Magician*, in which he caricatures Aleister Crowley.) In his novella *Death in Venice*, Mann picks up on the Hermes theme of psychopompos; he is a bit indirect yet unmistakably clear, thus creating a hermetic topos.

Otfried Preussler's *Krabat* (published in English as *The Curse of the Darkling Mill*), in no way a mere children's book as it is often regarded, has a lot to offer for the practicing magician or witch, which is why I have made it recommended reading among my coffee-party friends—and none of the ladies has regretted it yet. But Preussler is certainly not an occultist or a magician.

Piers Anthony topped the renowned *New York Times* bestseller list numerous times with his Xanth saga, and since then he has become one of the great names in fantasy literature—which does not stop him from sharply rejecting any type of occultism for himself.

Here we are dealing with authors who have no connection to magic whatsoever but are capable of dealing with magical, occult themes in a way that seems quite authentic to many people.

But let me finally get to my own opinion of Rowling and her Harry Potter epic, dear Juliane, even if I have the suspicion that you are not really going to like what I say. Luckily, I am no literary critic, so let me just put it this way: if Rowling really were a practicing magician, regardless of whether or not she had formal training in some kind of magical lodge, I feel she should have her pentacles ripped to pieces and her altar candles burned to the ground for what she has done.

Because what she describes in all love of detail is the sheer horror of every serious magician: a complete, self-governed, bourgeois, stuffy, overly human alternative world that is not one stitch better in its self-centered narrow-mindedness than the world of the Muggles themselves. Intrigues, games of power, humorless bureaucracy, and endless red tape (a Ministry of Magic—unbelievable!): what witch or magician in his or her right mind would voluntarily live in such a place?

And there we have it already—I think we have discovered the formula that the author uses to get such results. In short: "a topsy-turvy world." But that is about all. After all, there are no authentic magical insider techniques or other such information mentioned in these books whatsoever.

You already said yourself that Dumbledore could be straight out of a fairy tale. But that goes for all of the characters: the archaic fight between good and evil, themes such as betrayal and loyalty, stupidity and cleverness—all these and more can be found in an overabundant number of fairy tales and, of course, in their predecessors: myths and legends.

Then add a story of personal development; a few elements swiped from the books for young people written by Lewis Carroll, Enid Blyton, Astrid Lindgren, and the like; not to forget of course the stories of the Wizard of Oz—and poof! The never-ending story is complete! The use of a few magic spells and curses here and there, or standard magical utensils such as magic wands and robes, certainly does not require sound knowledge of the magic scene, and has about as much to do with it as the specialty magazines for stage magicians and illusionists. Anyone with a brain can make these kinds of things up with a minimum of research.

It may be difficult for the literary novice to comprehend how the literary or poetic craft is actually practiced. Since I have no intention of subjecting you to an essay here on creative writing, let it be sufficient to say that authors quite often fall back on older reference material before shaping and wording something in their own way in accordance with their personal writing style and the value system of their era. Let's just examine three of the books mentioned above more closely: there was plenty of older reference material for Goethe's *Faust*; Preussler retells an ancient legend in *Krabat*; and Piers Anthony falls back on various myths and fairy tales to give his novels the appropriate plot elements and the necessary magical touch. Principally, you are right: it really cannot just be made up. It requires a certain amount of literary skill—but no more than that.

Do not get me wrong, dear Juliane—this doesn't mean that we still cannot enjoy the Harry Potter books. Or that we should have to feel guilty for doing so.

Personally, I have never really had any interest in British boarding-school novels (and that is basically what these books are), but, while their mother was busy brewing up magic potions under strict observance of the phases of the moon and the planetary hours, I did have the honor of reading the Potter books aloud to my cheeky little nephews. A good way to expand one's knowledge, by the way. In any case, they both highly enjoyed the books, and I would not want to hold that against anyone. But please—do not mistake them for real magic!

In piteous supplication,
Your Aunt Klara

To Write to the Author

If you wish to contact the author or would like more information about this book, please write to the author in care of Llewellyn Worldwide and we will forward your request. Both the author and publisher appreciate hearing from you and learning of your enjoyment of this book and how it has helped you. Llewellyn Worldwide cannot guarantee that every letter written to the author will be answered, but all will be forwarded. Please write to:

Frater U∴ D∴
℅ Llewellyn Worldwide
2143 Wooddale Drive, Dept. 978-0-7387-1479-0
Woodbury, MN 55125-2989, U.S.A.

Please enclose a self-addressed stamped envelope for reply,
or $1.00 to cover costs. If outside the U.S.A., enclose
an international postal reply coupon.

Many of Llewellyn's authors have websites with additional information and resources. For more information, please visit our website at
http://www.llewellyn.com

High Magic
Theory & Practice
Frater U∴ D∴.

Magic may be one of the most difficult, diversified, and fascinating of all the occult sciences. Understanding the theory behind this rich Western tradition is crucial to becoming an accomplished magician. This comprehensive and well-rounded introduction to magical practice provides a solid foundation for furthering one's magic studies.

Instead of issuing spells and rituals like a recipe book, this magic primer explains the basic laws governing magic. The author also discusses what it means to be a "good" magician, emphasizing self-discipline and training one's will, imagination, and trance abilities. Many facets of high magic are covered, including the Lesser Banishing Ritual of the Pentagram, sigil magic, ritual magic, visualization, the Greater Ritual of the Pentagram, planetary magic, tools of the magician, trance work, and much more.

978-0-7387-0471-5, 432 pp., 7½ x 9⅛   **$31.95**

High Magic II
Expanded Theory and Practice
FRATER U.'. D.'.

Europe's best-known ceremonial magician and contemporary occult author, Frater U.'. D.'., is back with the companion volume to his highly acclaimed *High Magic*. Previously unavailable in English, this advanced guide to high magic has been eagerly awaited by ceremonial magicians, mages, and hermetic practitioners.

High Magic II explores the theory and practice of a variety of types of magic—including mirror magic, mudras, sigil magic, shamanism, magical orders, folk magic, demonic magic, divination, and letter magic. The book also delves into magic and yoga, magic in the Bible, the practical Kabbalah, forms of initiation, and the magic of ancient Egypt and the late Hellenistic period. Many provocative areas of magical practice are addressed, some of them for the first time in an English-language book.

978-0-7387-1063-1, 480 pp., 7½ x 9⅛   **$31.95**

The New Encyclopedia of the Occult
John Michael Greer

From *Aarab Zereq* to *Zos Kia Cultus*, this is the most complete occult reference work on the market. With this one text, you will gain a thorough overview of the history and current state of the occult from a variety of North American and Western European traditions. Its pages offer the essential knowledge you need to make sense of the occult, along with references for further reading if you want to learn more.

You will find the whole range of occult tradition, lore, history, philosophy, and practice in the Western world. *The New Encyclopedia of the Occult* includes magic, alchemy, astrology, divination, Tarot, palmistry, geomancy, magical orders such as the Golden Dawn and Rosicrucians, Wiccan, Thelema, Theosophy, modern Paganism, and biographies of important occultists.

978-1-56718-336-8, 576 pp., 8 x 10   **$32.95**

The Magician's Companion
A Practical and Encyclopedic Guide to Magical and Religious Symbolism
BILL WHITCOMB

The Magician's Companion is an essential reference book, overflowing with a wide range of occult and esoteric materials that are indispensable to anyone engaged in the magical arts.

The magical knowledge of our ancestors comprises an intricate and elegant technology. This book attempts to make the ancient systems accessible and useful to modern magicians by categorizing and cross-referencing the major magical symbol-systems (i.e., worldviews on inner and outer levels).

This comprehensive book discusses and compares over thirty-five magical models. Also included are discussions of the theory and practice of magic and ritual; sections on alchemy, magical alphabets, talismans, sigils, magical herbs, and plants; suggested programs of study; and much more.

978-0-87542-868-0, 608 pp., 7 x 10   **$29.95**

The Complete Magician's Tables
STEPHEN SKINNER

Featuring four times more tables than Aleister Crowley's *Liber 777*, Stephen Skinner's *The Complete Magician's Tables* is the most complete collection of magician's tables available. This monumental work documents thousands of mystical links—spanning Pagan pantheons, Kabbalah, astrology, Tarot, I Ching, angels, demons, herbs, perfumes, and more!

The sources of this remarkable compilation range from classic grimoires to modern theories of prime numbers and atomic weights. Data from Peter de Abano, Albertus Magnus, Cornelius Agrippa, and other prominent scholars is referenced here, in addition to hidden gems found in unpublished medieval grimoires and Kabbalistic works.

Well-organized and easy to use, *The Complete Magician's Tables* will help you understand the vast connections making up our strange and mysterious universe.

978-0-7387-1164-5, 432 pp., 7¼ x 10   **$49.95**

Foundations of Magic
Techniques & Spells That Work
J. F. O'NEILL

Is there a link between psychology and magic? Can the psyche have an impact on magical practice? *Foundations of Magic* is a unique beginner's guide to spellcraft that synthesizes ceremonial magic and proven psychological techniques to work everyday spells.

Without emphasizing any school of magic or belief system, this secular spell book is for people of all backgrounds. J. F. O'Neill introduces the basics of spellcraft and explains the psychological preparation needed to work magic. There are exercises for editing old memories and creating new ones, self-hypnosis, and reaching higher trance states. After becoming fully trained in the ways of magic, readers may begin working spells to find love, attract money, alleviate pain, achieve goals, eliminate depression, increase personal power, and more.

978-0-7387-0743-3, 264 pp., 7½ x 9⅛   **$16.95**

Postmodern Magic
The Art of Magic in the Information Age
PATRICK DUNN

Fresh ideas for the modern mage are at the heart of this thought-provoking guide to magic theory. Approaching magical practice from an information paradigm, Patrick Dunn provides a unique and contemporary perspective on an ancient practice.

Imagination, psychology, and authority—the most basic techniques of magic—are introduced first. From there, Dunn teaches all about symbol systems, magical artifacts, sigils, spirits, elementals, languages, and magical journeys, and explains their significance in magical practice. There are also exercises for developing magic skills, along with techniques for creating talismans, glamours, servitors, divination decks, modern defixios, and your own astral temple. Dunn also offers tips on aura detection, divination, occult networking, and conducting your own magic research.

978-0-7387-0663-4, 264 pp., 6 x 9 **$14.95**

Ritual Magic
What It Is & How to Do It
DONALD TYSON

For thousands of years men and women have practiced it, despite the severe repression of sovereigns and priests. *Ritual Magic* takes you into the heart of the entrancing, astonishing, and at times mystifying secret garden of magic.

What is this ancient power? Where does it come from? How does it work? Can it truly move mountains, make the dead speak, and call down the moon from heaven? Which part of the claims made for magic are true in the most literal sense, and which are poetic exaggerations that must be interpreted symbolically? How can magic be used to improve your life?

This book answers these and many other questions in a clear and direct manner, making sense of the non-sense. It also reveals the foundations of practical ritual magic, showing how the branches of modern occultism grew from a single root.

978-0-87542-835-2, 288 pp., 6 x 9   **$12.95**

Practical Magic for Beginners
Techniques & Rituals to Focus Magical Energy
Brandy Williams

We can all practice magic to improve our everyday lives. *Practical Magic for Beginners* is a straightforward introduction to magical practice for everyone.

This comprehensive training course presents the foundations of spellcraft and ritual magic through short and simple exercises. Readers explore their energy and senses, and then move on to developing skills in extrasensory perception, divination, and introspection. Magical timing, magical processes, ritual space and tools, journaling, and dreamwork are all explained and discussed in depth. This nondenominational guidebook also includes twenty rituals related to friendship, love, prosperity, health, and other common concerns.

978-0-7387-0661-0, 288 pp., 5³⁄₁₆ x 8   **$13.95**

Magic, Power, Language, Symbol
A Magician's Exploration of Linguistics
PATRICK DUNN

All forms of magic are linked to language. As a magic practitioner and a linguist, Patrick Dunn illuminates this fascinating relationship and offers breakthrough theories on how and why magic works.

Drawing on linguistics and semiotics (the study of symbols), Dunn illuminates the magical use of language, both theoretically and practically. He poses new theories on the mechanics of magic by analyzing the structure of ritual, written signs and sigils, primal language, incantations across cultures, Qabalah and gematria (Hebrew numerology), and the Enochian vocabulary. This revolutionary paradigm can help magicians understand how sigils and talismans work, compose Enochian spells, speak in tongues for magic, create mantras, work with gematria, use postmodern defixios, and refine their practice in countless other ways.

978-0-7387-1360-1, 288 pp., 6 x 9 **$17.95**

Inside a Magical Lodge
Group Ritual in the Western Tradition
JOHN MICHAEL GREER

Magical lodges are one of the most important and least understood parts of the Western esoteric traditions. The secrecy of
lodge organizations has made it next to impossible to learn
what magical lodges do, and has kept hidden their powerful
and effective traditions of ritual, symbolism, and organization.

This is the first book to reveal the foundations of lodge
work on all levels—from the framework of group structure that
allows lodges to handle the practical needs of a working magical group efficiently, through the subtle approaches to symbolism and ritual developed within lodge circles, to the potent
magical methods that lodges use in their ceremonial workings.

This book is a must-read for students of magical traditions,
for practitioners of other kinds of group magical work, and for
all who wonder about the hidden world behind lodge doors.

978-1-56718-314-6, 360 pp., 6 x 9   **$17.95**
